WHAT PEOPLE ARE SAYING ABOUT

HUNGRY CAPITAL

Luigi Russi takes un ⸻ *ıate the lives of people everywhere ir* ⸻ *¹ safety of our food. He brings insight* ⸻ *ociology and political economy to lini* ⸻ *with the appalling persistence and increa* ⸻ *malnutrition. A must read.*
Jayati Ghosh, ⸻ᴜressor of Economics, Jawaharlal Nehru University

This is a thought-provoking book on the food industries and how these are entangled with the world of finance. It is theoretically well grounded, original and rich in empirical detail. It is an important contribution to the international debate on the future of agriculture.
Jan Douwe van der Ploeg, Professor in Transition Studies, Wageningen University

Russi issues a stark warning, as he identifies how the drive for profits and the deregulation of commodity trading are re-shaping the business strategies of the large corporations who procure, broker and reassemble our food. The result is the acceleration of the ecological crises facing the food supply.
David Barling, Reader in Food Policy, City University London and co-author of *Food Policy: Integrating Health, Environment and Society*

At a time when finance and food are the epicentre of global crises, Luigi Russi's study provides a unique insight into the dynamics driving these complex but critical chains of human economic interaction. A must read for anyone analysing complex socio-economic processes and the potential for social progress.

Anastasia Nesvetailova, Reader in International Political Economy, City University London and author of *Financial Alchemy in Crisis: The Great Liquidity Illusion*

Luigi Russi has made a significant contribution to the unpicking of the relationship between finance and food by opening up for scrutiny the powerful and uncontrolled forces operating in this obscure and complex trading system, which has only just been recognised as giving rise to a crisis which is as potentially damaging as the failure to maintain control of the world's banking industry.

Peter Robbins, Author of *Stolen Fruit: The Tropical Commodities Disaster*

Hungry Capital provides a timely and novel analysis of the new frontier of financial capitalism.

Ole Bjerg, Associate Professor, Department of Management, Politics and Philosophy, Copenhagen Business School

Hungry Capital

The Financialization of Food

Hungry Capital

The Financialization of Food

Luigi Russi

Winchester, UK
Washington, USA

First published by Zero Books, 2013
Zero Books is an imprint of John Hunt Publishing Ltd., Laurel House, Station Approach,
Alresford, Hants, SO24 9JH, UK
office1@jhpbooks.net
www.johnhuntpublishing.com
www.zero-books.net

For distributor details and how to order please visit the 'Ordering' section on our website.

Text copyright: Luigi Russi 2013

ISBN: 978 1 78099 771 1

A CIP catalogue record for this book is available from the British Library.

Design: Stuart Davies

Printed and bound by CPI Group (UK) Ltd, Croydon, CRO 4YY

We operate a distinctive and ethical publishing philosophy in all
areas of our business, from our global network of authors to
production and worldwide distribution.

CONTENTS

For Putli

Acknowledgments

I have contracted many debts of gratitude in the process of writing this book. Over the last couple of years, I have had the opportunity to meet outstanding and exciting teachers at the International University College of Turin, City University London and Schumacher College. As far as the subject of this book is concerned, I am deeply indebted to Anastasia Nesvetailova, Colin Tudge, David Barling, Fabian Muniesa, Gunther Teubner, Jan Toporowski, John Haskell, Joseph Halevi, Luca Pes, Saki Bailey, Talha Syed, Tim Lang and Ugo Mattei. Other teachers have also illuminated my path with their thoughts and writings and provided support and encouragement: Jayati Ghosh, Jan Douwe van der Ploeg, Ole Bjerg, Peter Robbins and Robert Biel. I also wish to acknowledge the invaluable support of the friends that proofread and provided feedback on earlier drafts of this manuscript: Alfonso Javier Encinas Escobar, Vico Belli and Ishupal S. Kang.

The ideas presented in *Hungry Capital* have benefitted from exposure at academic venues around the world. In particular, I am indebted to Jayati Ghosh and Rajendra Kundu for having me present the book at Jawaharlal Nehru University, and to Surajit Mazumdar for putting together a seminar at Ambedkar University Delhi. I also wish to thank Deigracia Nongkynrih, Bhagirathi Panda (and Danny Pariat) for arranging a talk at NEHU. In addition to that, Giuseppe Mastruzzo, Michele Spanò and Antonio Marchisio have made it possible for me to partake in the IPEL Seminar Series at the International University College of Turin, and Steffen Boehm and Ann-Christine Frandsen have selected my work for presentation at the 4th Critical Finance Studies Conference at the University of Essex. I am grateful to them all.

Furthermore, this book would have never seen the light, had it not been for the generous financial support I have received over the years. The Fondazione Giovanni Goria and the Fondazione CRT have kindly sponsored my studies at the International University College of Turin through their "Master dei Talenti della Società Civile" project. My doctoral studies at City University London have been made possible by the generous support of the Bank of Italy, which has funded my first year with a "Donato Menichella" scholarship, and of the Fondazione Felice Gianani, which has provided further funding for the second year through a "Borsa di Studio 'Felice Gianani'." Of course, it goes without saying that any and all ideas expressed in this book are mine only, and shouldn't be taken to reflect the views of my institutional affiliations, sponsors or academic network. I equally take sole responsibility for any mistakes and/or inaccuracies that may be left in the text.

In addition to the above, I have benefitted from further support from many other sources. I am grateful to Mary-Jayne for being close at a crucial time, to everyone at the Calthorpe Project for bringing me closer to the soil, to Roberto Schellino for sharing glimpses of peasant life, to Looby, Klaudia and Stefan for introducing me to permaculture, to Alice for making me discover the world of food, to David, Ann and Ghan for offering a quiet place and West Country landscapes and to everyone at the ILSC and Goodenough College for providing such a supportive environment.

Once again, I find myself short of words to express the unconditional love and support I have received from my parents, Elvio and Flavia, and from my brother Guido. Thank you for believing in me and supporting my choices in uncertain times. Thank you also to my acquired family for welcoming me so warmly and providing moments of respite from the hum of work: Danny, Deanna, Richard and Zelma.

The beauty, elegance and hearty laughter of Putli fill my life with color. I am honored to have you in my life, and I love you. This book is for you.

List of Abbreviations

AoA: Agreement on Agriculture

CAP: Common Agricultural Policy

CFTC: Commodity Futures Trading Commission

CSA: Community-Supported Agriculture

GATT: General Agreement on Tariffs and Trade

IBC: Instituto Brasileiro do Café

OTC: Over-the-Counter derivative

SAPs: Structural Adjustment Programs

TNC: Transnational Corporation

TRIPs: Agreement on Trade-Related Aspects of Intellectual Property Rights

WTO: World Trade Organization

Introduction: Beholding Monstrosity

Fig.1 Title-page of Hobbes's *Leviathan* (detail)
Source: Rare Books and Special Collections Division of the Library of
Congress, Washington, D.C.

The relationship between food and finance can best be introduced through a metaphor, by reference to a picture found on
the cover of the original edition of Thomas Hobbes's *Leviathan*.[1]
The latter is a depiction of a giant, whose body consists of a
mosaic of individual people "stuck" together into the larger
structure of Leviathan's anatomy. In the context of Hobbes's
work, the Leviathan represents the sovereign, whose authority
originates from a social contract between individuals, all wishing
to escape a state of nature characterized by aggressive competitive relations. In a postmodern world, of course, Hobbes's

retreat into a "state of nature" of relentless competition between individuals, as well as the exclusive endowment of agency upon humans, make his ideas somewhat obsolete to the critical observer.[2]

Leaving Hobbes's ideas aside, however, the same figure of the Leviathan displays features that are strikingly essential for conceptualizing the world of finance, and its relation to the production and consumption of food. First, the mosaic-like nature of the monster stems from its being an entanglement featuring multiple sources of agency.[3] These are caught in a network where they cling to one another by mutually constraining and orienting the range of options available to each. Second, it combines a horizontal, network-like web of actors that somehow "stick" together, with a vertical division between a core (the head) and a periphery (the limbs). The Leviathan of food and finance is therefore a complex creature which displays apparently contradictory features: decentralized agency across a network in combination with core-periphery arrangements that suggest some degree of centralization; a multiplicity of actors alongside the apparent unity of the system. In this respect, the intricacy of the Leviathan metaphor finds its best conceptual counterpart in the idea of Empire. This concept, first introduced by Michael Hardt and Antonio Negri,[4] has been defined as a network that arranges "the social and the natural world through the assembling of resources, processes, territories, people and images into specific constellations that channel wealth towards the centre."[5] In this respect, Empire allows to reconcile the insight that the financial pressures confronting the world of food have an impersonal, systemic hold, with their emergence from complex patterns of agency. This is precisely the insight that this book attempts to explore.

There is no shortage of accounts of the food economy in contemporary literature that address it as part of the "system" of capitalism. Indeed, these appear to enjoy wide currency, particu-

larly in the political economy of food camp. A central characteristic of such accounts is to posit structural trends to which the
food economy is subject. However, there also appears to be an
increasing space for theories that posit a kind of mutual
causality.[6] Within this stream, the food economy is not just an
appendage of the wider capitalist machine, but plays a defining
role in shaping the latter. What financial capitalism "is," in other
words, is co-determined by how it is assembled within the
modern food economy.

In this book, I suggest that it is a combination of these two
approaches that allows one to obtain a comprehensive picture of
the relationship between food and finance. On the one hand,
finance can be characterized as a system, the evolution of which
lends itself to be described in the terminology of structural
accounts. On the other hand, however, the boundaries of that
system are—upon closer inspection—constantly shifting and
demarcated by in-between fields featuring multiple forms of
agency. And these agencies can be pinpointed as they shuffle into
new combinations.

To translate this debate with reference to the food-finance
relationship, it is possible to pay heed to accounts that evidence
that a transition is underway in the modalities of capital accumulation within the food economy. These accounts underscore the
independent role of finance in affecting the dynamics of
production and consumption, bringing about the "financialization" of the food economy. At the same time, if one attempts
to trace this predominance of finance with specific reference to
the food system, one is confronted with a multiplicity of possible
pathways to be followed. What one finds along these pathways
are strings of actors that do much more than simply obey
financial imperatives, but are actually engaged in what Bruno
Latour calls "world-making."[7] In the case of food, this world-
making is most evident in the ways "food" is assembled, disas-
sembled or outright withdrawn. So, for example, the progressive

industrialization of production chains makes it so that "food" comes to include things like margarine (though the examples could be many more), which are really the outcome of a process of industrial assembly of "natural" inputs. Or even like Parmalat's *latte fresco blu*, where the engineering of a new product is guided by financial imperatives. On the other hand, "food" disappears into a piece of paper or an electronic recording as it is traded as a commodity on financial markets.

Such pathways are the subject of exposition in Chapters 4 to 7. These chapters look—in sequence—at the speculation on commodity markets, the "engineering" of food production through the operations of transnational corporations entangled in a web of financial transactions, and the phenomenon of land grabbing. Chapter 6 offers a case study of the coffee value chain, where several of these issues play out simultaneously. These chapters offer an idea of the systemic reach of financial pressures, by situating such pressures inside the diverse entanglement of actors that contribute to shape the world of food.

The first two chapters, instead, carry more of a theoretical bent. They present arguments to reconcile the two perspectives mentioned earlier. The first perspective focuses on a structural reading of the financialization of the food economy, in which the relationship between food and finance is posited in terms of core-periphery or system-environment dynamics. This is complemented by the second perspective: an object-centered approach focusing on the mediations performed by heterogeneous actors entangled in situated networks. The combination of these two approaches is meant to allow the reader to behold the majestic monstrosity of the relationship between food and finance. As the boundaries of food production come under pressure and are shifted and redrawn to accommodate increasingly complex forms of agency, the self-referentiality of an unstable financial system is projected onto the world of food, while the increased fragility of the food economy feeds in turn the very chaotic features of the financial system. Giving rise to a gigantic Leviathan that holds itself together while, at every step, risks to crumble.

2

Finance: Systemic Complexity, Complex Agencies

When discussing finance, it is commonplace to treat it as some sort of entity upon which this or that characterization can be pinned. For instance, depictions of finance as "speculative" or "extractive" assume precisely that there exists such a thing as finance. If finance is understood in this way, it then becomes relevant to ask questions about its relationship with other such entities, such as "the 'real' economy" or—as this book does— "food." Now, of course, if one allows oneself to open the black box of this thing called finance, what he/she will find is a complex entanglement of actors (human and non-human, which may in turn reveal themselves as complex entities upon closer inspection) as well as practices linking such actors in ways which may be more or less stable.

These two kinds of intuitions, namely that finance is endowed with some unity—and can therefore be studied as a "thing"— while simultaneously displaying an important degree of multiplicity, are the two trails that I will develop in this chapter. At first sight, these different perspectives might seem irreconcilable. However, I wish to illustrate how combining them can offer a picture of the relationship between food and finance that retains some of the complexity of the situated worlds in which "it" is assembled, tracing the steps through which a panoramic endowed with some degree of systematization is stabilized. It is—in other words—by looking at how structures and "orderings" are achieved and assembled that it becomes really possible to grasp how "systematic processes [...] *become* systematic."[1]

The task at hand will require me to initiate a conversation

between different brands of scholarship: a task that will make this chapter somewhat reliant on technical terminology (notwithstanding my effort to keep this to a minimum). This has been balanced by providing succinct overviews of the theories that will be used, insofar as they may be relevant to the understanding of the contribution that each brings to the conversation. Housekeeping notices aside, this chapter develops in three sections. First, it introduces the idea of finance as a complex system. This perspective discloses possibilities like self-referentiality (whereby finance constitutes a closed loop out of touch with the "real" economy) and financial expansionism (understood as the progressive obliteration of alternative ways of assembling and "processing" the world). The second section looks instead at finance in the making, i.e. as it is recursively assembled through the mediation of complex forms of agency spanning both the human and non-human camp. Finally, the third section traces lines of communication and possible complementarities between the two approaches, through the argument that it is by following situated actors in their assembling of worlds (the work undertaken in the second section) that the trends of finance as a system (discussed in the next section) can better be grasped and explained.

The Systemic Complexity of Finance
Introducing Systems

The first intuition that I am going to develop is one that has a long history, namely that capitalism as a system (including in its present "financial" phase) is driven by endogenous tendencies that—for better or for worse—have a decisive impact on the structuring of economic relations. It is the very idea of a "system" that implies an openness to the possibility that problems arising within the system be a product of the system's own forces.[2]

Understanding how it becomes possible to appraise

capitalism through this lens requires a brief introduction to the concept of "system." In a very simple sense, a system is any collection of elements organized in a particular way. Central to the idea of a system, in particular, is more the organizational aspect ("organized in a particular way") than the elements of which it is comprised: the *patterns of relations* that bind the elements together are what ultimately defines the system.[3]

Borrowing from biological models, the German systems theorist Niklas Luhmann stated that the systems from which what we call "society" is held together[4]—and which he called social systems—consist of webs of relationships, relationships which Luhmann named "communication events." In his framework, these webs—as if cast from a spider—would be strung out across a substrate of "anchor points." These "anchor points" are where individual actors can be found: on the borders of a web of communication,[5] yet—as outlined by later commentators of Luhmann[6]—in a position subtly to affect the layout of the web that clings to them.[7]

The relationships from which social systems emerge are "communication events." A communication event is simply the name for a connection that successfully manages to structure expectations about what is possible within a shared space.[8] So, for example, the customer's announcement that he/she is willing to enter into an economic transaction is understood by the seller once the customer brings the goods to the till. This connection narrows down the possible operations that can take place in this shared space to—in this case—payment for the goods. In other words, "communication events" successfully delimit the type of operations that may take place within a shared space, so as to enable performance of a particular task or function (such as an economic transaction) through the deployment of a specialist code.[9] And in so doing, they establish the conditions for a build-up of exchanges centered around that task, precisely by regulating expectations about what is possible within the space, so as to provide a "structure" for further communications.[10] Since systems arise from chains of communication events, communication of—say—an "economic" nature in turn gives rise to a "system" of economic relations.[11] The same reasoning could be further repeated to define—for example—the political, legal or mass media systems.

The distinctive character of a system arises from the particular "code" that guides the sequence of communicative events within that system. So, for example, communication events of a "legal" nature would connect with the purpose of determining the legality/illegality of some other event and, in so doing, generate "law." Hence, legal/illegal would be the code of the legal system. Similarly, economic communication is concerned with questions of proprietary access to scarce resources, as articulated through the medium of money.[12] In fact, as "every transfer of goods and services involves a counter-transfer of money,"[13] the problem of scarcity is reduced to monetary terms.[14] Hence, the binary of payment/non-payment is what ultimately qualifies a transaction as an "economic" one, by regulating access to resources through willingness and ability to pay.[15]

What a system "does" is typically referred to as its function, even though that need not imply some teleological purpose in a human sense, and is actually better appraised *ex post*, by looking at how the system behaves.[16] Referring to this concept in order to underscore the existence of different social systems such as politics, law, the economy and the mass media, Luhmann used the word *functional differentiation*.[17] Central to Luhmann's description of a plurality of functional systems consisting of communicative events is the abandonment of the idea that society consists of a collation of human beings: these appear instead to be entangled in a web of communicative relations over which they have little control upon.[18]

For a pattern of relations to constitute itself as a system, it is important that it leads to the emergence of the twin properties of *operational closure* and *selective openness*. In a very simple sense, they could be summarised as follows: operational closure describes the separation of a system from what is outside of it (its "environment"). Yet, a system—while "closed off" from the environment—remains susceptible to environmental stimuli that it will process according to its own code (selective openness).

Luhmann defined operational closure as the onset of a "self-reproducing network which relies exclusively on self-generated information and is capable of distinguishing internal needs from what it sees as environmental problems."[19] In simple terms, this means that the relations binding together the system's elements connect in a recursive manner only with other relations of the same kind. When such a degree of differentiation is achieved, the system becomes operationally closed. For instance, within the economic system, only "economic" communication is able to connect with "economic" communication, whereas communication of a non-economic nature cannot relate directly to the latter: the economic system effectively runs itself. Of course, regulatory measures or political statements can affect the economy indirectly (as a consequence of the other feature mentioned above: selective openness). However, they cannot directly bring about a particular outcome. They can, instead, simply "irritate" the economy (from the outside), attempting to "nudge" it in a certain direction: the final outcome will still depend solely on how the economic system "processes" such external stimuli.[20] It may make it easier to visualize an "operationally closed" system as a cell that is separated from the "outside" by a membrane, making it so that whatever happens inside is a "cellular" operation, and whatever is left outside is the cell's "environment."[21] As a consequence of a system's operational closure, a distinction is therefore drawn between "it"—the system—and the environment in which the system is immersed, i.e. everything lying outside of the system.[22]

The other property of a system is that—while being operationally closed—it still remains selectively open to perturbation from the environment. In other words, although the environment cannot communicate directly with the "inside" of a system (direct input), the latter can nonetheless be perturbated by events occurring in the environment. The difference between direct input and perturbation is that, in the former case, the environment could directly determine a particular outcome in a straightforward cause-effect relationship.[23] In the case of operationally closed systems, however, any perturbation that stimulates the system will ignite a chain of internal operations the outcome of which cannot be determined *a priori*. The system, in other words, will process any outside stimulus according to its specific binary code by stripping it of any "noise" that does not fit the system's parameters. As a consequence, it will react to what it makes of that external event after "digesting" it through its binary code: external causes will not trigger system responses directly, but rather after "[i]ncoming messages or inputs are sorted, sifted, evaluated and recombined before they are [...] translated into action."[24] To refer back to the earlier example: the selective openness of the economic system enables it to "take in" external stimuli in the form of—say—regulatory measures. However, by virtue of the economy's operational closure, any such stimuli do not directly interfere with the working of the economy, but are subservient to the economy's own "code" that will act as a filter between—in this case—the law and chains of economic operations.[25]

Feedback and Entropy

In the previous paragraph I have discussed the general idea of a system as a network of relations displaying the twin properties of operational closure and selective openness. These features configure systems as *self-regulating* entities. What this means is that systems possess the ability to respond to perturbations from their environment in ways that aim to preserve the continuity of the pattern from which the system arises.[26] In other words, a system will make adjustments—either to its internal configuration or by perturbating its external environment—which are aimed at restoring a previous balance which had been attained between itself and the outside. This process is known as *negative feedback*.[27] It may however occur that perturbations in the environment do not lead the system to a stabilizing correction, but rather ignite what is known as a *positive feedback* process, whereby the system's reaction further compounds the environmental conditions from which the original perturbation arose. Through this reinforcing feedback, a persistent mismatch between the system's internal requirements and the surrounding environmental conditions will lead either to the attainment of new, more sophisticated equilibria through a growth in complexity of the system's organization, or otherwise to runaway dynamics that will lead to the unravelling of the system.[28]

What "balance" means in relation to system-environment interactions can fruitfully be understood by reference to the second law of thermodynamics. The latter states that, whenever a system is closed (i.e. it entertains no relations with an environment), it will become progressive more disorderly (or "entropic"—entropy meaning simply a loss of structure). Now, we know that systems are endowed with a degree of openness which enables interactions with an environment to take place. So long as the environment is able to offer resources for the system to function and absorb any dissipations stemming from the system's internal processes, the system will be able to preserve its internal order: system-building therefore appears as a fundamentally anti-entropic phenomenon.[29] When, however, the relationship between system and environment becomes such that the latter can no longer "fuel" the system and/or can no longer recycle the byproducts of the system's internal metabolism, the web of relations that characterize the system's "openness" towards the environment unravel and the former becomes isolated and exposed to a progressive increase in internal disorder (according to the second law of thermodynamics), leading eventually to the unravelling of the pattern of relations from which it originates.[30]

Finance as a System

Whereas the previous paragraphs have focused on systems in general, this section hones back in on the main topic of this chapter, namely finance. Within systems scholarship, there exists a debate as to whether finance can be regarded as an autonomous system nested within the economy, with which it interacts, albeit always following its own internal logic. In order to understand whether finance can be characterized as a system, it is important to establish that it instantiates a pattern of recursively connected communicative events that displays "operational closure" vis-à-vis the larger economic system.[31]

In this respect, it has been observed how financial communication no longer uses payments *as a means* to regulate access to scarce resources, in order to arrange provision for future needs.[32] Instead, payments are effected *only* with a view to elicit further payments, without any reference to the possession/nonpossession of resources: it is no longer just a matter of monetizing resources, but rather one of monetizing money. Or, to put it in another way, finance no longer mirrors economic fundamentals, but rather behaves as a "hall of mirrors" reflecting each other.[33] This feature of finance capital has been depicted in some sociological literature as an alteration of the traditional profit-making cycle, whereby profits are made through the production of goods or services. Instead, it has been argued that money circulates on financial markets with the only purpose to generate more money.[34] Supporting this position is the observation that financial instruments such as derivatives even rely on a novel conception of "property" as no longer bound to production, but simply as an appropriation of the "fluctuations in isolated aspects of an asset's value in and of themselves."[35]

One can therefore witness an important innovation in the code of the financial system: payment/non-payment is no longer a placeholder for the problem of scarcity and proprietary distribution of resources, but becomes purely self-referential, so that payments are triggered by other payments, without acting as a measure for the transfer of goods and services.[36] This altered binary code also fosters innovation at the level of the medium through which the code is administered.[37] As mentioned earlier, in the economic system the medium of communication is money.[38] In an economic transaction, *what* is traded against money does matter since—without it—there would equally be no payment. In the context of an economic transaction, therefore, money simply offers a standardized shorthand to reduce to quantitative expression all goods and services, with a view to facilitate exchange.[39]

The medium through which financial operations unfold, instead, takes the "compressi[on] [of] contexts of meaning"[40] enacted through money one step further, by also enabling a distancing from economic fundamentals. This, in turn, is necessary for chains of financial flows to build up into a self-referential orbit. In this respect, it has for example been suggested that the vehicle mediating communication at the financial level ought to be one that "holds itself up," by autonomously originating further financial flows,[41] thereby enacting "a certain kind of self-reference."[42] This is a property that applies to derivative instruments. A derivative is simply a security, the value of which is related to the price volatility of an underlying asset, which does not—however—have to be owned to profit from its fluctuations.[43] Because derivatives tailor their own exposure to the volatility of the underlying asset—by specifying the dimensions across which their value may change in response to that of the asset—they are sufficient, in and of themselves, to define the structure of any further financial flows originating from them,[44] so that they effectively "hold themselves up."

But there is more. In fact, they seem to display another important property. Namely, when derivative trades are considered as a lattice of interlocked transactions, they form a mesh in which any barriers between different forms of capital are broken down, since it becomes possible to "take the attributes of a range of different asset types and put them together" in some derivative product.[45] Bryan and Rafferty[46] provide the example of convertible bonds, which are bonds that are convertible into shares, thereby "blending" equity and debt and overcoming their fragmentation into different classes. Furthermore, convertible bonds establish price relations between different forms of investment (equity and corporate debt), and in turn foster competition in the rate of return between them. Another, slightly different, example is that of commodity index funds. These funds—which will be analyzed in greater depth in Chapter 4— issue shares (or other financial instruments, like a swap), the returns on which are linked to an index (i.e. a basket) of commodity prices. As a consequence, commodity index funds "blend" heterogeneous commodities (including edible commodities such as wheat or coffee), by turning them into largely fungible assets that are only relevant as reference points on which to peg further payments. Furthermore, through such indices, assets with largely unrelated economic fundamentals (for example, wheat and gas) are packaged into a new financial instrument. From which it follows that their performance relative to one another now acquires relevance inside that instrument.[47]

Two conclusions are possible at this point. First, derivative instruments originate a system where the recursivity of financial flows is enabled through the "homogeneization" of different forms of capital, which are "flattened" into largely fungible reference points on which to build further flows of payments.[48] In the financial system, in other words, considerable autonomy is obtained from economic fundamentals, precisely because different forms of capital — turned into generic "assets" after being "digested" in a mesh of derivative instruments — can be readily substituted for one another, so that the continuity of payment flows is unbroken by the heterogeneity of the underlying economic entities (*what* sets off payment flows is removed from the underlying economic specificities).[49] Second, thanks to a web of derivatives providing a common metric to compare different forms of capital, otherwise heterogeneous assets are consequently subject to heightened competitive relations as their performance relative to one another is now comparable.[50]

In the end, therefore, it seems that the binary code of finance is characterized by a self-referentiality of payments. The latter connect to each other endogenously, irrespective of the specifics of external economic processes, since these are largely interchangeable in financial terms. This is facilitated by a new medium coming under the guise of derivative instruments that — as a system — enable direct commensuration of different asset classes and heightened competition for profits. If this view is correct, it would go a long way in explaining the discrepancy between "real" growth rates of the planet's GDP of about 3 to 5% annually and the much higher expected rates of profit on financial markets. This discrepancy, in particular, can be seen as the resultant of a new set of financial relations that no longer mirror and facilitate market competition, but actually compound it. In particular, the lattice of derivatives requires a restructuring of underlying assets to live up to the pressures of financial profitability,[51] in ways that do not (and cannot, if the "real" GDP is only a fraction of profits expected on financial markets) add any value, but simply extract it from the outside (understood as labour or the natural ecosystem) or redistribute it through the zero-sum games that are financial bubbles.[52]

Systemic Addiction and Expansionism

In the last paragraph I have presented some arguments in favour of the characterization of finance as a new social system that is embedded within—yet autonomous of—the "real" economy. I wish to take this discussion of finance as a system further, and relate it to the phenomenon of destabilizing positive feedback which may affect system-environment relationships. Runaway self-reinforcing dynamics may occur whenever "a solution to a systemic problem reduces (or disguises) the symptoms, but does nothing to solve the underlying problem."[53] This phenomenon has been brought to the fore—in relation to social systems—by scholars such as Gunther Teubner[54] and Robert Biel.[55]

For Teubner, the self-referentiality of social systems entails a risk of expansionism. In other words, systems routinely project their internal code upon the environment in an attempt to strip external inputs of complexity and make them "processable" in terms of the system's code.[56] For Teubner, it is a danger when this mode of functioning gets out of hand and acts on the environment in a way that makes it exclusively subservient to the system's reproduction—in what has elsewhere been defined as a "grinding up of structure"[57]—so that the former's resilience to the system's demand for its resources is crucially depleted. When this happens, in other words, the system has entered a growth dynamic that prevents the attainment of a sustainable, symbiotic equilibrium with the environment, leading instead to the colonization and eventual depletion of the latter.

Teubner further contextualizes this argument in relation to the economic system, and asks whether the creation of money create a compulsion to grow in the real economy, igniting an "accelerating growth spiral"[58] that deploys itself through a comprehensive commoditization of its environment. As a consequence, the environment becomes less able to reproduce itself, sheltered from the strain the system's functioning imposes on it. This basic intuition can readily be applied to the financial system and its autonomization from the "real" economy through the onset of a web of derivatives. In fact, because the flows for which derivatives provide a self-propagating infrastructure are ultimately flows of money,[59] the latter act like RNA-sequences, "conveyor belts" set in motion between the two systems, enabling financial growth dynamics to reverberate across the economy.[60] In light of this, an issue can be raised as to whether the self-reproduction of the financial system ignites a positive feedback cycle, that affects the economic system in ways that make the latter function unsustainably.

Positive feedback need not always translate into runaway dynamics that lead to the depletion of the environment and the eventual unravelling of the system. Instead, they can lead to "learning" and the attainment of new *plateaus* of stability in system-environment relationships. Indeed, an entire academic approach—that of the French "régulation school"—is focused on studying the shifts in capital accumulation regimes corresponding to different patterns of system-environment relations.[61] According to this school, every "regime" is characterized by relatively stable modes of capital accumulation supported by a specific institutional structure.[62] Therefore, regimes can—in a systems perspective—be understood as consolidated patterns in the interaction of the economic system with the extra-economic environment on which it depends. Transition between regimes occurs as the result of the unravelling of previous equilibria and the attainment of new *plateaus*.

In this perspective, Biel contends that—up to the 1980s—the "regime of accumulation" was such that it was possible to shuffle entropy away by increasing the dependence of the economic system on the environment thanks to the "a still-dynamic neo-colonialism in the periphery and [...] practically unlimited plundering of the ecosystem."[63] From the 1980s onward, however, these possibilities have decreased both in scope and quality due to the environment's diminished ability to regenerate "virgin" spaces and fresh ecological resources open for capitalist commodification. In this changed context, new patterns of system-environment interactions are needed. However, thanks to the role of financial capital in accelerating the growth dynamics inherent in the economic system, a more aggressive colonization of the natural environment and of non-commodified spaces of relation is taking place, as opposed to a slowing down and internal reconfiguration to make room for the emergence of more sustainable alternatives. So, for example, by stimulating the "restructuring" of corporate assets to keep revenues flowing, financial capital encourages an extraction of profits from the bodies of workers through "layoffs, casualization and outsourcing."[64] Similar restructurings appear to be occurring in relation to newly peripheral countries, as exemplified by the budget policing imposed through conditional lending on countries like Greece, Portugal and—most recently—Spain, facing an attempt to open their veins in a manner analogous, for example, to Latin America in the 1980s.[65] Financial capital seems, in other words, to feed on the very entropy that the economic system creates and to accelerate it, thereby preventing the attainment of new, more sustainable equilibria and igniting runaway dynamics.[66]

However, the financial system is problematic beyond reducing the durability and resilience of the economic system through the encouragement of unsustainable growth that depletes whatever resources—natural or informational—the environment has to offer. Indeed, finance appears to display its own endogenous form of instability that makes it prone to frequent crashes that drag down—with it—the credit system on which the economy relies.[67]

In particular, the development of derivative finance comes with an illusion of greater "liquidity," as an increasing range of risks are priced and allocated by creating markets around previously "illiquid" assets.[68] A paramount example is that of derivatives on sub-prime mortgages: as the risk of default was made tradeable through (derivative) securities—the value of which depended on the cash flow arising from bundles of mortgages— a class of assets that banks were previously forced to hold on their balance sheet (i.e. mortgages) was mobilized on financial markets.

However, in case markets for such instruments dry up (as in the case of the subprime mortgage crisis, as soon as news of large amounts of defaults on mortgages came home to roost), the assumed "liquidity" of derivative instruments vanishes and large numbers of financial operators that accepted these in exchange for money proper are confronted with the prospect of not holding enough "liquid" assets to face payments.[69] In this sense, the autonomy of the financial system from the "real" economy attained through the development of a web of derivatives is a Trojan horse. While it generates apparent "liquidity" by mobilising previously incommensurable types of capital, it also makes the system as a whole vulnerable to liquidity crises and domino effects that may cause the credit system to grind to a halt, with repercussions for the real economy.

Complex Agency in Financial Networks

So far, I have developed the intuition that "financial capital" can be conceptualized in terms of systems, in order to articulate the kind of impersonal embrace that it appears to exert on other entities like the "real" economy. In this section, instead, I seek to increase the complexity of the foregoing picture by "zooming in," so as to recover a sense of how the relations from which a system is built up are established and maintained over time through the interplay of a wide set of "actors," both human and non-human. This in order to avoid the rabbit-in-the-hat trick, whereby a "system" is derived from nowhere.[70] My hope instead is to gain a sense of how "finance" as a system does not just "exist," but is actually enacted through a recursive weaving of relations featuring a motley crew of human bodies, objects, practices as well as silent spatial and cognitive "backgrounds." For this purpose, I will try to bring into focus some of the complex forms of agency that (1) enact finance as a self-referential system and (2) shape the relationship between finance and the "real" economy.

Finance as an Entanglement of Agents

In a seminal study on the role of objects in financial markets, MacKenzie draws attention on the interaction between human and non-human agents.[71] For Latour, the role of non-human agents is to increase the durability of patterns of relations by crystallizing them in a material medium.[72] In this respect, the equipment adopted by operators on financial markets is often telling in its ability to highlight practically how the self-referential character of financial communication is enacted and facilitated.[73]

In particular, it is worthwhile to bring into focus some of the mechanisms through which the "virtuality" that is often ascribed to finance is actively created. So, for example, Hessling and Pahl[74] point to a study of the "micro" practices through which a "global" financial market is achieved.[75] That study, in turn, shows the importance of face-to-screen interactions after the onset of screen-based dealing in the early 1980s.[76] A new community of time and space is enacted precisely through the face-to-screen orientation of traders working in financial markets, whose bodies have to gather additional capabilities such as "broker's ear"[77] to be able to retain awareness of the physical environment of the trading room in which they are immediately located.[78] Through face-to-screen interactions and exposure to a stream of data, building on which both monetary and informational exchanges take place between traders, "the market" is actively established as an entity.[79] Indeed, one cannot overestimate the importance of advances in information and communication technology in giving durability to the relations on which a "global" market is built. This is further demonstrated by the progressive replacement of slower media like the telephone precisely for their inability to allow the dissemination and processing of ever larger amounts of information.[80]

At the same time, the complexity of a "global" market is achieved at the cost of simplifying the information that is circulated across it down to single price figures.[81] Indeed, the adoption of standardized and abstract representations of the economic realities to which financial trades refer to is a condition for the viability of large-scale exchanges performed at a distance.[82] An example of this comes in the form of standardized paper claims to commodities in transit; a feature pointed to me by a former commodities trader.[83] Another mode through which "virtuality" in the face of "real" economic processes is enacted is, for example, through the use of entries in electronic databases, which standardize and facilitate the circulation of inputs from the economy in the form of prices.[84] As a consequence, great effort goes into the transformation of "inputs" from the economy into financial "facts," in order for them to connect to the ongoing flux of financial transactions.[85] The figures so obtained are, in turn, what guides the making of transactions across this space, enacting precisely the particular form of recursivity from which a self-referential system emerges.

The speed and capillarity with which information is disseminated may lead one to think of financial markets as deterministic machines, where sequences of financial transactions criss-cross in seemingly automatic and effortless fashion. However, Leyshon and Thrift[86] enrich the picture by drawing attention to the fact that the increasing amount and speed of information circulating across financial networks is, actually, a great source of uncertainty and — as suggested by Knorr Cetina and Bruegger[87] — also of price volatility. It is a common experience that decisions become harder the more information one has available. The same goes for financial transactions, which require the sieving of meaning from an increasingly rich and complex array of data. As a consequence, the very ability of financial transactions to build on each other in recursive sequences appears itself to be quite the achievement, by successfully binding the agency of both human and non-human actors into a common assemblage.

This is made possible by specific technical arrangements. So, for example, the prevalence of technical analysis over fundamental analysis reported by Hessling and Pahl[88] is one of the tools through which the self-reference of communicative events, from which the autonomy of finance as a system emerges, is achieved. To be clear, fundamental analysis is a form of analysis of financial data predicated on observation of the underlying economic fundamentals, and it is a translation of the efficient-market hypothesis, whereby prices factor in all available information about economic fundamentals.[89] Technical analysis is, instead, a form of forecasting whereby information on previous trends in the market is used to foresee future fluctuations. In this type of analysis, therefore, previous trading patterns are thought to affect future trading patterns.[90] One of the most interesting exemplifications of this, which I have come across personally, is the use of autoregressive statistical models in financial forecasting. Such models forecast future price trends based upon "lagged" (i.e. past) data on the trading of a particular instrument.[91] In so doing, therefore, these statistics—as shown more generally by Didier[92]—express chains of financial transactions as related to one another, thereby contributing to assemble them into a system.

It is also not uncommon that financial market operators act on price models in such a way as to build "automatisms" in the behavior of the market.[93] The most common example is the case of options pricing using the Black-Scholes model.[94] Widespread use by financial operators made the predictions of the model accurate, because the market crucially included actors "equipped" with charts obtained from the Black-Sholes model. Finally, beyond the use of analytical equipment that introduces some degree of stability to the unfolding of financial operations, the outright replacement of human agency with automated trading by pre-programmed software introduces a further dimension of machine-to-machine communication that builds further recursivity in financial transactions.[95] Automated trading also highlights the process of simplification of inputs coming from the "real" economy for the purpose of financial trades, as these inputs are reduced to "ghostly images that symbolize buying power."[96]

In conclusion, the above discussion offers a flavour of how the working of financial markets, far from being a purely deterministic machine, is actually practically achieved through clever attempts to automate payment decisions based on past payment decisions, enacting a recursivity that is essential to the emerging of finance as a self-referential communicative system.[97]

Finance and the "Real" Economy

If finance is an autonomous system that unfolds in relative autonomy vis-à-vis the "real" economy, the same argument can be turned on its head in order to affirm a degree of autonomy of the real economy with respect to financial dynamics: "inputs from the financial environment have to pass the filters of the economic organizations and vice versa."[98] Therefore, in order to shed light on the influence of the financial system on the economy, it is necessary to turn one's attention to the selective networking taking place at the edges of different function systems. In particular, despite each following its own recursive, self-referential logic, the financial and the economic system remain open to one another through the weaving of relations taking place in in-between fields of actors that, by "[c]ombining different logics of actions, [...] mediate between autonomous function systems."[99] In this respect, such networks feature entities like accounting standards that streamline the provision of financial information, coupled with technical elements like spreadsheets, to which other forms of background agency also ought to be added, such as business cultures, flexible time-space configurations and even adequate management bodies.

As regards the role of accounting practices and their deployment through spreadsheets, the latter's ease of use coupled with the ability to provide standardized financial information that displays characteristics such as "generality, comparability, balance, coherence, and simplicity"[100] loads spreadsheets with "rhetorical energy"[101] and persuasive power in shaping the decisions of managers about corporate strategy. It is, therefore, no exaggeration to say that spreadsheet number-crunching has become—aided by the standardization of accounting practices—the dominant act of speech in some corporations,[102] enabling better comparability with competitors.

Of course, the strength of such connection—far from being a feat accomplished in isolation—ought to be understood against a whole space of other practices and understandings[103] that put the use of spreadsheets and accounting standards into a broader *financial culture of business governance*. Such a culture of financial governance has been documented for example by Salento and Masino,[104] who describe a transition towards centralization coupled with management protagonism, requiring that company managers both hold the corporation under tight control, as well as display immediate receptivity to changes in the value of company stocks: "companies need to communicate *'activism'*."[105] The expectations defining this type of management culture arise not just as a matter of belief in the particular discourse of, for example, maximization of shareholder value. They rely, instead, on a silent background featuring, for example, innovative management bodies. Indeed, the ability of managers to keep the company under their reins and steer it through the sea of financial imperatives comes to be embodied in new "techniques of the self" which managers ought to be equipped with,[106] such as a penchant for creative interaction, a sensitivity to anomaly, as well as the ability to weave powerful narratives of change through enhanced storytelling. In an analogous manner, the ability of firms to alter their configuration globally so as to respond swiftly to changes in the financial tide is reflected in new configurations of the very space of business, through—for example—an increase in global mobility on the part of company executives that are always "on the go." Another example lies in the very arrangement of offices, with the disappearance of assigned spaces and the introduction of "touchdown" areas for managers, where they coalesce to engage in collective problem solving.[107] The extreme example of this new trend in the localization of business is offered by a firm providing consulting solutions for company management. In its office, all that consultants have is a trolley, with workspace being booked in a "just-in-time" logic.[108]

These details about the role of bodies and the definition of business localities constitute non-representational backgrounds, i.e. set-ups of practices and spaces that operate beyond the dimension of discourse and ideas, affecting conceptual symbolizations indirectly by working on the "subtext."[109] Their importance should not be underestimated. In fact, another ethnographic study of investment bankers highlights the importance of specific matter-of-fact circumstances in shaping a particular discourse of adherence to the dictates of the financial market. So, for example, bodies that are always alert and able to keep apace with the community of "Wall Street time" through—for example—constantly checking BlackBerry phones, around-the-clock workdays and an emphasis on constantly updating one's resume as a way to be always ready for the next career move form the "subtext" to the (conceptual) discourse of maximization of shareholder value.[110] Furthermore, the conception of the "market" as an ever-shifting frame that commands immediate adaptation (a conception which is subsequently acted upon by investment bankers) appears to be crucially affected by the fragmented time horizon that comes to be accepted within their community, through the shared experience of downsizing. Against a background where downsizing is understood as a challenge that increases fitness and ability to thrive by promoting an "internalized sense of hyperefficiency and extreme responsiveness"[111] (a process that is also facilitated by a set of institutional arrangements in the investment banking sector, such as remuneration levels that accommodate for frequently being in and out of jobs), new identities are assembled that are the ultimate embodiment of the need for speed in corporate decision-making.[112] Subtly enough, the entanglement of investment bankers in this background of practices and time-spaces affects their stance towards downsizing in the wider corporate world, making the maximization of "shareholder value"—as represented through the figures of stock prices—the embodiment of their wider set of cultural and ethical commitments.[113] Downsizing, in fact, is understood to exert the same fitness-inducing outcomes in the larger corporate workforce, portrayed as prey to a sluggish routine and therefore in "need [of] a jolt of downsizing."[114]

In sum, the financial style of management appears to be immersed in a background of practices which regulate expectations around—for example—management bodies, business localities and the temporal horizons of corporate strategy and it is aided by key pieces of equipment like accounting standards and spreadsheets. In this sense, therefore, it becomes clear how the channels, through which "financial motives"[115] come to impinge on the functioning of the economy, display the traits of a complex assemblage that is asserted through recursive performance.

The centrality of financial outcomes to corporate decision-making emerges out of an ordering that is less coherent than it might at first seem. Indeed, some of the managers interviewed by Salento and Masino[116] show a clear ambivalence towards financially-driven short-termism that puts corporate executives under unrealistic demands about keeping the reins of a company which they are forced to steer in sometimes contradictory directions for the sake of financial performance. This conclusion lends credit to the fact that, while it is indeed plausible to speak of "capture" of the economy by the logic of finance, such an assertion cannot be made in a deterministic fashion.[117] "[B]y crossing the borders [between finance and the economy], causality gets fractured,"[118] meaning that the routes through which finance nudges economic activity are—as this section has shown—more unusual and less coherent or one-way than the discourse of maximization of performance on the stock market may lead one to believe. At the same time, one cannot overlook the complex set of agencies at play in order to stabilize the integration between financial motives and corporate performance. These entanglements of actors are what makes it possible to even speak of a financial "capture" of the economy.[119]

Conclusion

This chapter has offered a sketch of the relationship between finance and the economy, through the different—but complementary—perspectives of the systems approach and actor-network theory. In brief, the following arguments have been made:

1 Finance can be conceptualized as a self-referential system through the recursive occurrence of transactions building solely on previous transactions.

2 The financial system has developed its own binary code, which differs from that of the economic system. In the economic system, the binary payment/non-payment mediates questions of proprietary access to scarce resources for the provision of future needs. In the financial

system, instead, such a reference to productive needs is obliterated, and an autonomization from questions of ownership is sought.

3 The autonomy of the financial system is also achieved through a new medium of communication in the form of derivative instruments. Not only do these redefine the idea of "property" so as to limit it to changes in the value of a particular underlying asset. In addition to this, derivatives also enable convertibility and comparison between assets of different kinds and with different degrees of "liquidity." In this respect, they standardize different expressions of capital and enable wider competition around profitability.

4 While autonomous from the economic system, the system of finance still retains important points of contact with the economy. Through these openings, the financial system is able to compound the instability of an increasingly entropic economic system—which relies more and more on the colonization of its environment to preserve itself[120]—with its own unstable dynamics coming from the dilution of liquid assets in the portfolios of financial operators, as a consequence of financial innovation.

5 Finance as a system does not arise from nowhere. Instead, it is the product of a complex socio-technical network featuring, for example, information technologies, analytic techniques and standardized representations of economic realities that facilitate the transmission and processing of information within the system.

6 Similarly, the "capture" of the economy on the part of the financial system is not the outcome of a deterministic process. This "capture," instead, appears more like a sharing of calculative practices and informational devices, as well as the resultant of a background of management cultures and practices.

In light of this, it seems plausible to characterize the financial system as a reflexive process. The concept of reflexivity in the world of finance has been analyzed in some depth by Soros,[121] and it is perhaps best summarised—at its most general—as follows: if we understand the financial system as an assemblage of different forms of agency, these hold together through the repeated "rehearsal" of incomplete scripts which are honed and refined over time. The financial system imposes itself as an "entity," which constrains actors scattered in a network, but it simultaneously originates *from* the forces deployed by the latter within "financial" networks.[122] This is on display in the earlier example of investment bankers. It is from their agency that a particular relationship between corporate strategy and financial markets is enforced. Yet, they act the way they do after experiencing the market as an external force, with attributes which they claim to understand better than the average worker. In this case, the market is both something they experience as external to their actions, as well as something they actively shape through their practices, offering perhaps the clearest illustration of the circularity that characterizes finance as a reflexive process: it reproduces itself through the enactment of limited and open-ended scripts by a wide variety of agents.

For the purpose of the discussion of the influence of finance on the food system, these insights are perhaps the most relevant ones. On the one hand, finance is a process that shapes its environment in order to enforce compliance with its particular internal code: this aspect is the focus of most of this book, and the next chapters hone in precisely on this process, from turning food into just another tradeable commodity mobilized on financial markets, to the progressive extraction of value from the food chain in order to carve new spaces for corporate profit. On the other hand, however, one must not overlook the fact that the very reflexivity of finance as a process scattered between multiple sites is what allows "glitches" to happen. These glitches can be seen as "the escaping edge of any systemization or economization,"[123] as windows of opportunities that are opened within a recursively assembled process. Therefore, despite the capillary influence that finance appears to exert across all areas of the food economy, the possibility of enacting alternative production and consumption networks in the cracks of the modern food system offers fertile opportunities for resistance to the "financialization" of the food economy,[124] some of which will be briefly reviewed in the concluding chapter.

3

The Financialization of Food: An Overview

In the previous chapter, I highlighted how the autonomization (and indifference) of the financial system with respect to the dynamics of production has exacerbated unsustainable interactions between the economy and its social and natural environment. These, in turn, have put the latter under increasing pressure, a pressure that has started to become apparent at several points during the 1970s and the 1980s.[1] As a consequence, one witnesses today a more aggressive subjugation of the environment within which the economy reproduces itself, through a re-engineering of extra-economic relations to make them fit the particular requirements of the economic system's reproduction.[2]

The set of relations clustered around the production and consumption of food traditionally display features that cannot be described in purely economic terms,[3] but which outline— instead—an organic relationship between man and nature, capable of balancing out "environmental and economic risk and maintain[ing] the productive base of agriculture over time."[4] In this context, I am using "organic" as a shorthand to refer to the interdependence between the two terms of the relationship, as embodied in traditional forms of co-production binding human labour and design with natural productivity.[5] These features, as enacted in smallholder agriculture (albeit in ways that have changed over time, making the peasant condition an evolving concept that does not merely rely on a romantic veneration of an idyllic past[6]), have typically enabled to cater for the nutritional needs of human communities, while simultaneously enabling the reproduction of ecosystems around the world.[7]

Under the aggressive expansionism of the "financialized"

economy, however, the richness and diversity of the assemblage of extra-economic relations that constitute the "outside" of the economic system has come under renewed pressure. In particular, it has been threatened by an ongoing re-engineering to enable continued extraction and dissipation from the economic system, to escape the fate of systemic entropy.[8] This, of course, has also affected the world of food.

In this area, in particular, "economic expansionism" has been articulated through the accommodation of an increasing number of actors that—by sliding in between producer-consumer relationships—have reorganized them in such a way as to enable an increasing degree of extraction of profits. It is with these "middle spaces"[9] that the following chapters are concerned. In this introductory part, I wish however to offer a more general framework within which to situate the sort of assemblage that the food economy has become today, providing a blueprint for understanding how financial speculation, industrial food chains laid down by transnational corporations and land grabbing are to be placed in relation to one another.

Food Regimes

The framework that I propose in this chapter builds on what is known as "food regime" theory. In Chapter 2, I have discussed "regime theory" in relation to the evolution of system-environment relations within capitalism at large. Food regime theory represents, instead, an adaptation of that framework to the world of food. Given the focus that has been placed here on systems and the relationship with their environment consisting of extra-systemic relations, "food regime" theory appears to be the most suitable point of departure.

In relation to food, the evolution of the uneasy relationship between the economic system and the set of more-than-economic relationships governing the co-production of man and nature has been conceptualized in terms of a struggle between peasant agriculture—where the calculus of production is only part of a larger struggle for increased resilience through stewardship and care for the natural resource base[10]—and attempts at re-wiring agriculture in a purely economic perspective. In particular, proponents of the "food regime" approach have so far outlined two main phases through which this process has unfolded until the 1980s.

The first food regime goes from the end of the nineteenth century up until the first World War. Until then, trade had mostly taken place within a hierarchical colonial ordering, with colonies providing raw materials to fuel the industrial production of the metropolitan centers. This remained mostly the case in relation to tropical commodities also during this period. However, the defining aspect of the first food regime is the onset of trade relations between states according to the logic of competition (not colonization) and the early development of an agro-industrial complex. Indeed, in this period white settler nations like Canada, Australia, New Zealand, the United States and Argentina began to produce commodities (like wheat and meat) that were also produced in temperate countries. These exports were, therefore, in competition with agricultural production in the Old World and indeed displaced European agriculture.[11]

Although the basic unit of production in the white settler countries was the family farm (developed by the formerly displaced peasants left landless by the British enclosures), the development of smallholding outside of a pre-existing set of peasant relations adapted to the new territories made agriculture in these countries more open to the penetration of capital since the beginning,[12] through, for example, the introduction of chemical use and machinery.[13] The early integration of commercial agriculture with industrial capital spurred the development of industry in exporting countries. Therefore, the white settler countries became the first to feature economies organized at the national level as a mixture of industry and (commercial) agriculture.[14]

The first food regime also offers a taste of the extent to which the onset of industrial capitalism brought with it early attempts at restructuring peasant co-production. In fact, the introduction of industrial inputs "streamlined" settler agriculture so as to provide wage foods for the workers in the industrial centers in increasingly cost-effective ways.[15] In turn, these technical changes began to open up the relationship of interdependence between man and nature that is central to peasant farming. They did so by replacing some of the biological inputs that would normally be reproduced on the farm within the traditional model of mixed farming (where—for example—farm animals would produce manure to fertilize the fields), so as to allow extensive monocultures.

The second "food regime," which is typically placed after the hiatus of the two world wars, is characterized by a further encroachment of the logic of economic production on more-than-economic relations of co-production. In particular, the new food regime was characterized by a comprehensive industrialization of agriculture with a view to maximizing food production. This was made possible by the combined use of a mix of industrial inputs, hybrid seed varieties, monoculture and irrigation.[16] However, the increasing integration of agriculture into the industrial complex has not just taken the form of the "appropriation" by industrial capital of phases of the production process (what has been called by some scholars "appropriationism"[17])— e.g. through the provision of chemical inputs. Instead, it has also featured the inclusion of agricultural produce within large processing chains that reduce what were previously final products into mere inputs. At its strongest, this tendency—called substitutionism[18]—has taken the form of a direct substitution of agricultural inputs with synthetic ones. Margarine, a known butter-substitute, is often presented as a typical example of substitutionism, where the "link between the final food product and the original, easily identifiable agricultural raw material"[19] has been severed through the selection of cheaper agricultural products (such as vegetable oils) used merely as inputs for a product that is assembled industrially.

A second salient trait of this food regime is the active role of states in promoting and protecting domestic agriculture. This resulted, in particular, in the production of huge surpluses in the United States, but also in Canada and in Europe. Such excess production was often dumped in the developing world under the guise of food aid, as a strategy to open new export markets, as well as to ward off the advancement of Communism during the Cold War.[20] Part of the same strategy—feeding Third World nations in a bid to counterweight Soviet influence—was the export of "industrial" techniques of crop cultivation, based on extensive use of external inputs in the form of pesticides, herbicides and fertilizers, monocultures, irrigation methods and hybrid seeds that thrived in conjunction with chemical inputs. This effort has gone down in history under the name of "Green Revolution."[21]

In sum, this regime stepped up the marginalization of the peasantry, already visible during the first food regime, through a further industrialization of agriculture, both by means of engineering cultivation methods through industrial inputs, as well by wedging new stages of processing between farm production and final consumption that would absorb shares of the final price.[22] The export of "technified" agriculture to the Third World under the aegis of the Green Revolution contributed to the further marginalization of the peasantry there as well, as smallholder farmers were unable to access the new technologies, were unable to compete in an increasingly harsh environment and were ultimately driven off the land.[23]

Of course, the abandonment of peasant forms of co-production—whereby the natural productivity of the land and its ability to reproduce itself are highly valued—led to an increasing ecological and economic fragility of agriculture as a whole. This fragility was incurred in a bid to dissipate the contradictions of industrialization—in the form of huge masses of urban poor in need of feeding—through a "push" on the planet's carrying capacity by adopting a "productionist" solution[24] that absorbs the question of feeding the world entirely into a push for more yields.[25] The results of this process have come home to roost during the oil crisis of the 1970s. During that time, in fact, increased oil prices, among other concurrent factors, fed into increased food prices (and shortages) due to the tight linkage of agriculture with industrial production methods requiring fossil fuel use.[26] Furthermore, the dependence on food imports by Third World countries—which had been set up in previous years precisely through the channel of food aid—confronted them with higher export bills that eventually led to the default of several countries in the late 1970s.[27] The oil shocks and Third World debt crisis subsequently sparked a transition to the current "third" food regime, in an effort to push even further the ongoing disciplining of relations of co-production of man and nature, as a way to keep sustaining a fragile industrialized food system.

The Third Regime

The Third World debt crisis was caused by abundant loans being made available to Third World countries to finance their imports. The money for such loans came from oil exporting nations, that accumulated dollar reserves during the oil price hike of the 1970s. The Third World debt crisis occurred, therefore, through the failure of the Bretton Woods system, which—put in place after World War II—consisted of an international governance regime for financial flows through, for example, strict capital controls.[28] This system collapsed precisely because of the onset of a market for dollars from oil export revenues, which made it impossible to keep financial flows under control.

Simultaneously, the bankruptcy of Third World countries offered the platform on which to establish a new regime of accumulation in these changed circumstances.

In fact, Third World countries were "bailed out" from international financial institutions like the World Bank and the International Monetary Fund on condition that they undertake "structural adjustment programs" (SAPs) aimed at restoring these countries' productivity (according to the particular economic theory that these institutions were pushing, based on maximum free trade). These SAPs often required a rapid withdrawal of state intervention and an opening up of countries to foreign trade. In relation to trade in agricultural commodities, this led to the promotion of export crops (with which to earn foreign currency to pay for imports) in Third World countries that, as will be shown in Chapter 6, would lead to an export glut and to chronically low prices.[29, 30]

Furthermore, in 1994 the Agreement on Agriculture was approved as part of the Uruguay Round of international trade negotiations that gave rise to the World Trade Organization. The World Trade Organization has its origins in the GATT, an agreement sealed in the postwar period to bring about a more open international trading environment through the lowering of tariffs. In 1994, the GATT was incorporated in the World Trade Organization along with a host of other agreements, including the Agreement on Agriculture (AoA); the WTO's institutional task being to administer and assist in the development of the legal framework outlined by the existing agreements.[31] The AoA was meant to gradually phase out agricultural subsidies through which developed countries were protecting their domestic systems from foreign competition. However, the agreement has been recognized as insufficient to bring any meaningful reversal in a general trend that sees developing countries forced—for example through SAPs—to open their own economies to foreign commodities, while unable to penetrate foreign developed markets that remain substantially closed.[32] Last, but not least, the WTO agreements of 1994 also included an agreement on Trade-Related Aspects of Intellectual Property (TRIPs), which contained provisions for the patentability of plant varieties, offering the required legal infrastructure for the development of genetic biotechnology,[33] despite criticism that it would contribute to transform farmers "from producers into consumers of corporate-patented agricultural products."[34]

Against this institutional setting, the third food regime has taken on the following features:

1 Increasing weight of financial capital, through either the direct entrance of financial actors in the food business, or however a change in the operations of food corporations towards the optimization of financial performance;[35]

2 The growth—thanks to the wide liberalization of markets—of multinational corporations, not just in the sector of food trade and processing, but also in the chemical inputs business and—most importantly—in the retail sector;[36]

3 The growth of genetic biotechnology, as aided by specific legal mechanisms such as legal protection for plant varieties as enshrined in the TRIPs agreement;

4 Increasing diversity in consumer choice, met by retailers through strategies of "global sourcing [...], product differentiation [...] and product innovation"[37] in a bid to reshape pathways between producers, processors and consumers with a view to mine value from a new economy of quality.[38]

The variety of traits displayed by the current state of the food economy, while somewhat puzzling at first, can be said to shape an "imperial" food regime.[39] The chief characteristic of this food regime is the aggressive projection of the calculative practices of a "financialized" economic system onto the set of natural and social relations governing food production, in ways that enable a higher streamlining of the latter for the purpose of extracting (financial) value. In particular, it can be said that—rather than promoting a re-thinking of system-environment relations towards greater sustainability—the financial system locks the production of food tighter into a global panopticon, where it is tied up in a matrix of largely interchangeable assets that become candidates for aggressive restructuring in order to match returns available elsewhere.[40] In other words, "the production, processing and distribution of food are […] re-patterned into a worldwide vehicle for generating cash flows to meet the highly elevated levels of expected profitability."[41] This re-patterning proceeds through the institution of "middle spaces," new forms of agency (e.g. financial markets or transnational corporations) that re-work previously existing arrangements in food production.[42]

The food system is a complex pattern of relationships that mobilize different entities and bind them together through connections of both an economic and more-than-economic nature. In the modern food regime, such relations are viewed merely as "a bundle of resources which provide opportunities for a quick profit."[43] As a consequence, this process generates tensions that take the shape of new forms of resistance aimed at preserving the relationship of co-production with natural ecosystems that has carried the food system along until now. In this respect, these struggles can be broadly characterized as attempts to preserve or re-instate peasant relations[44] and which are—to a large extent—the very symptom of the upheaval that is affecting the present food regime. They show the discontent associated with the current agrifood paradigm that, while still using hunger as a banner, leads instead to the subordination of food production to the logic of financial profit. From this follows that, despite there being enough food for everyone in the world,[45] the inequalities caused by this logic end up causing that very hunger and malnutrition;[46] as shown by the 2008 food price crisis, or by the "food deserts" caused by the expansion of supermarkets. Food struggles, in other words, ought to be understood as a defining element of the expansion of a liquid empire of capital.[47]

In light of this, it is possible to come back to the original image of the Leviathan. The relationship between food and finance appears today as a complex assemblage where every element is patterned in such a way as to take its place in a global machine that generates profit for the sake of profit. In so doing, however, it compromises the very ability of the environment of social and ecological relationships that sustain it to re-generate itself, coming dangerously close to a state of increasing entropy. At the same time, the aggressive assemblage that gives rise to the Leviathan of "financialized" food is contrasted by processes of resistance that seek to reclaim and/or remove the "middle spaces" through which the coercive ordering of capital is enforced.[48]

The remaining chapters delve further in the structure of this monster, by looking at the agency of financial markets in relation to commodity trade (Chapter 3), the agency of transnational corporations in re-patterning the production of food with a view to maximize financial performance (Chapter 4) and at a case study of coffee where processes of economic-driven re-patterning and commodification can be observed alongside attempts of resistance through—for example—the implementation of "fair trade" networks. Chapter 5 looks instead at the large-scale acquisition of land as a final stage in the re-ordering of productive relations, whereby land is mobilized as yet another asset. Finally, Chapter 6 summarizes the main arguments of the book, and focuses more closely on the options available to counteract the ongoing modulation of the food economy according to financial criteria.

4

Commodity Speculation

The fragility of the current food economy, and the role of finance in compounding such fragility with its self-referential dynamics of expansion and contraction, finds its clearest exemplification in the 2007-08 world food price crisis. Starting at the end of 2007, commodity markets witnessed an increase in the prices of major food commodities. These included both staple grains like rice, wheat and maize,[1] but also cash crops like coffee.[2] They peaked during 2008, generating waves of hunger in countries where a sizeable fraction of people's incomes is spent on food,[3] and subsequently petered out towards the end of that year. A similar rise in food prices has occurred from the end of 2011,[4] reaching worrying levels at the time of writing.[5]

The debate following the 2008 food price crisis has sparked wildly diverging opinions. A series of factors relating to the "economic fundamentals" of food production have been pointed at as possible culprits. Such factors include bad harvests and/or decreasing yields (e.g. due to soil depletion caused by increased fertilizer use), increasing competition between food crops and biofuel plantations, oil prices and increased demand for livestock fodder (consisting of grains) as a consequence of increased meat consumption in countries like India and China.[6] While the role of market fundamentals cannot be ruled out as such, the exclusive focus on "external" forces in producing the food price shock can be criticized for turning a blind eye on the endogenous dynamics of financial contraction and expansion.[7] It is these dynamics which this chapter brings into the spotlight, in relation to the wider framework of understanding outlined in the previous chapters.

Hedgers and Arbitrageurs

Commodity markets are simply spaces where deliverable goods are traded; as such, commodities are a category extending beyond agricultural products, including oil and gas.[8] Although physical delivery forms part of the definition of a commodity, this does not mean that the only allowed commodity trades are those for immediate delivery (also known as "spot" trading). In fact, it is precisely out of the need to shelter one's supplies or sales from the fluctuations of "spot" prices that derivative instruments made their appearance in the world of commodities. So, for example, a company producing bread might be willing to purchase today, at a set price, a certain amount of grain for future delivery. The contract by which this result would be obtained is called a *forward*. The benefit of this operation would be that the company could "lock in" the cost of its anticipated demand for a raw material it knows it will need in the future.[9] Similarly, a grain producer might want to undertake an obligation to deliver a certain amount of his/her production at a future date for a set price, so as to stabilize his/her income flow and have some figures on which to base a calculus of future production. Initially, such contracts would be made on an *ad hoc* basis, meaning that their precise content would be determined according to the needs of the parties. As the volume of traded commodities rose during the second half of the nineteenth century,[10] however, the need to allow bulk trading on exchanges featuring many different participants brought with it a tendency towards the standardization of derivative contracts, which pre-specified the type of commodity as well as the delivery date.[11] These standardized contracts allowing to buy and sell commodities for future delivery are called *futures*.[12]

In traditional markets for commodity futures, two main types of actors would typically be seen at work: hedgers and arbitrageurs. Hedgers would be those operators trading in derivatives to protect themselves against future price fluctuations for business needs. This is where the bread-making company and the grain manufacturer of the earlier example would fit. Next to them, one would find arbitrageurs (or "traditional" speculators). These would not be interested in the physical delivery of the commodity at a future date. Therefore, they would act on the market by undertaking commitments that would cancel each other out.[13] So, for example, one could commit to future purchase of grain at, say, $100, and then make a profit by exploiting subsequent price fluctuations that allowed to undertake a future sale at, say, $105; this buy-and-sell strategy that profits from increased prices is called *going long*.[14] Alternatively, a traditional speculator might sell before buying. This is possible because futures contracts simply entail an obligation to buy and sell at a future date, and do not require ownership of the physical asset (so long as one does not hold them until delivery comes due).[15] Hence, an arbitrageur can promise to sell grain at a future date (at a time when he/she expects the trading price to be higher than it would be, were he/she to undertake the same commitment at a later time, when the delivery date is closer) and then promise to buy it closer to delivery date when trading price has gone down. In the end, the two obligations cancel out and all the arbitrageur is left with is the profit from selling high and buying low—a strategy called *going short*.[16] In order for one to be successful in this type of arbitrage, possessing information on the underlying supply dynamics of the commodity would be key.[17] Furthermore, the presence of arbitrageurs on the commodity futures market would create an ongoing stream of participants willing to buy and sell futures, thereby guaranteeing the possibility for hedgers to find a counterparty with ease.[18]

Index Speculators

The progressive deregulation of derivative commodity markets gradually enlarged the camp of participants uninterested in taking delivery of physical commodities, well beyond traditional arbitrageurs. Whereas the number and size of speculators was originally constrained by regulatory limits on the amount of contracts they could hold, the situation changed during the 1990s. At that time, in fact, some actors obtained significant exemptions from the U.S. Commodity Futures Trading Commission (the regulatory body entrusted with supervision of commodity futures exchanges), allowing them to increase their position on the market.[19] Among such actors were merchant banks like Goldman Sachs, which enacted a revolutionary scheme that would prove to be one of the main contributing factors to the food price shock of the late 2000s.

In the early 1990s, in fact, Goldman Sachs came up with the idea of creating a commodity index fund. A commodity index is simply a mathematical formula in which the prices of different commodities are factored in according to different weights.[20] As a consequence, the value of the index can be thought of as the price of a basket of commodities, held in different proportions. Furthermore, under the assumption that the prices of futures reflect—at maturity—prices experienced on the spot market, indexes typically take as reference the price of the nearest-expiring futures contract.[21] Assuming futures prices later transfer over to the spot market, then the index can still be said to track commodity prices movements over time.[22]

This remark leads to the basic idea behind a commodity index fund, which is to replicate ownership of a basket of commodities so that "an investor theoretically experiences the same [financial] consequences as one who would have owned the corresponding commodities over the period of investment, and then selling them at the end of the period."[23] The way this is done is through a "swap" contract. A swap is simply a contract whereby two parties agree to exchange cash flows.[24] In a commodity index swap, an institutional investor like a pension fund agrees to pay the swap dealer (who is typically a merchant bank) the three-month Treasury bill rate, plus a management fee. In return, they will be credited with the changes in the value of the index over the agreed period of investment.[25] Hence, the investment tracks variations in the price of a basket of different commodities, essentially mimicking ownership of those commodities. Since the bank is committed to delivering returns replicating "synthetic" ownership of a bundle of commodities, it is necessary for it to balance this liability through an investment strategy that will match the index's performance. Now, since the index is obtained by combining a basket of commodity futures prices, the "natural" hedging strategy for the bank is simply to hold futures in proportion to the index's composition: any increments in the value of the index will be matched by increases in the value of the futures the bank holds in its portfolio. Directly holding positions that follow the index puts the bank in the condition to transfer any increases in the value of the index over the stipulated period to the institutional investor, in exchange for the three-month Treasury bill rate plus a management fee.

A significant issue arises here. In fact, while the index is an ongoing investment, futures—by their very nature—expire at a certain date into the future.[26] As a consequence, the bank will have to periodically "lengthen" its futures exposure to contracts with a later maturity date. The way it does this is by evening out the commitment to buy with a commitment to sell, thereby offsetting its exposure to futures nearing maturity. Furthermore, it will also open—on the "buy" side—new positions with a later maturity date.[27] The need periodically to "roll over" expiring commitments into others with later maturity dates arises purely from the bank's contractual commitment to deliver returns on the index. Hence, it will carry out such task regardless of the underlying market conditions.[28] This, as shown later in this chapter, has significant consequences.

Speculation After the Year 2000

Despite Goldman Sachs making index speculation available

already in the early 1990s, it was only after the year 2000 that this type of speculation gained momentum, to the point that—in 2008—about 40% of all open positions in the commodity futures market had come to be held by index speculators.[29] The reason of this tidal change in the weight of index speculation is to be found in a landmark regulatory development that occurred in the U.S. Indeed, 2000 is the year in which the Commodity Futures Modernization Act was passed. To understand the import of the Act, it is first of all necessary to introduce the idea of over-the-counter (OTC) derivative. This is simply a derivative contract that is not standardized and cannot, therefore, be traded on an open exchange, but is instead stipulated by interested parties in an *ad hoc* fashion.[30] The Commodity Futures Modernization Act allowed over-the-counter derivatives to trade in commodities, outside of the supervision of the U.S. Commodity Futures Trade Commission (CFTC). In essence, this meant that OTC derivatives could be entered into freely, without any need to disclose information to a regulatory body.[31] Furthermore, it became equally possible for parties uninterested in hedging for commercial purposes and only interested in speculation to enter into OTC commodity transactions.[32] These changes opened the floodgates of commodity markets to institutional investors with large amounts of money to park. And their influence came to be felt precisely through the mainstreaming of OTC instruments like index swaps that, by enabling the business of commodity index funds, changed the face of speculation on commodity markets. Index speculation later took more refined forms, such as that of commodity exchange traded funds (ETFs). Unlike commodity index swaps, which are OTC derivatives negotiated bilaterally between a bank and an institutional investor, commodity ETFs issue shares that are traded on the stock exchange and make commodity investment accessible also to a retail clientele. From the point of view of their effect on the commodity market—which is discussed in the next section—

they can however be considered equivalent to funds established through commodity index swaps.[33]

The liberalization of commodity speculation after the year 2000 also increased the range of speculators that would take both short and long positions in an attempt to arbitrage on price volatility, in much the same way as a "traditional" speculator would.[34] However, unlike a traditional speculator, these "money managers"—typically featuring hedge funds[35]—would trade with little regard to the underlying economic fundamentals, and resort instead to some of the techniques outlined earlier in Chapter 2—such as econometric forecasting based on past values of a given commodity—to identify and exploit price trends in commodity markets, as well as in other asset markets.[36] Because money managers actively manage a diversified portfolio, in which commodities feature alongside other assets, some of the positions they adopt on commodity markets are a consequence of events occurring in other exchanges: which explains recent findings that commodity prices have come to be increasingly correlated with each other, as well as with those of other types of asset.[37]

The increased presence of speculators of the latter kind—who attempt to profit from market volatility—has also been described as a further side-effect of index speculation. Index speculation— as I explain further in the following section—induces price dynamics that are unrelated to market fundamentals. Consequently, futures markets are less able to function on information about economic fundamentals and this uncertainty translates into increased volatility that, in turn, attracts participants like money managers, who are interested precisely in exploiting "price swings rather than fundamentals."[38]

Commodity Index Speculation and Escalating Commodity Prices

In the commodity futures market, the relation between the "spot" price (for immediate delivery) and the futures price is typically that the former will be greater than the latter.[39] More generally, sales further into the future will be carried out for less than if they were carried out closer to the present. As a consequence, if one plotted the price for a particular commodity, say wheat, starting from the "spot" price, then moving onto the price of the nearest expiring future, then to the second-nearest expiring future, and so on, one would theoretically see such figures arranged along a downward-sloping curve, meaning that prices get lower as the maturity date is pushed further into the future. This condition is typically referred to as *backwardation*, and it reflects the basic nature of a futures contract as a form of insurance against future price fluctuations. In order to protect oneself from such fluctuations, a premium is paid in terms of a lower price than one would receive by trading on the spot market.

There is, however, a second possibility. It can, in fact, happen that the price for future sale of a commodity exceeds that of a spot transaction. This situation is called *contango*. While, in theory, this should be an anomaly on commodities markets, it has actually been the norm during the 2008 world food price crisis. As futures prices exceed spot prices, this may lead to a hoarding of supplies (to take advantage of future increases in price) and to a surge in demand (to take advantage of the lower current price), thereby exacerbating scarcity in the affected commodities and driving up also their spot price.[40] In other words, in a *contango* market, futures prices may drive up commodity prices in a kind of self-reinforcing loop.[41]

In relation to this phenomenon, Frenk and Turbeville[42] eloquently argue how commodity index speculation plays a decisive role in "nudging" commodity markets towards contango. At the same time, it sends all the wrong signals to actual suppliers and consumers of the commodity, with the chance of creating a situation of induced scarcity that—in the

2008 crisis—led to such hardship as to prompt the peoples of several countries to take to the streets. The way this comes about is precisely because of the need, for the banks that are party to a commodity swap deal, periodically to roll over expiring futures contracts into longer-dated ones.

When markets are in contango, this means that—on "roll time"—banks will offset their position in the near-dated future at a lower price than the cost of taking a position in a contract expiring later. In other words, they will lose money. However, the cost of this is not actually felt by the bank, but it is charged back to the original investor as a "management fee."[43] The cost of rolling over in a contango market detracts significantly from the returns investors may otherwise obtain from a commodity's increasing price, as captured by the commodity index.[44] Despite this, increasing commodity prices have been a powerful lure for investors seeking an easy way to diversify their portfolio, especially following the dotcom and the housing price bubbles.[45] Furthermore, the passive nature of commodity index investment forgoes the need to appoint and monitor a dedicated trader, with the swap dealer-bank taking care of the periodic roll.[46]

Because index speculators routinely roll over their contracts at set times during each month, as well as because of the sheer turnover involved in this operation, it occurs that: (1) the nearest-expiring future becomes relatively underpriced during the roll period due to a surge in supply from index investors to offset their outstanding positions, whereas (2) the later-expiring future becomes relatively overpriced, again because of a surge in demand from index speculators. The simultaneous price depression of near-dated futures and inflation of far-dated ones is precisely what nudges commodity futures markets towards contango. This dynamic is further exacerbated by the trades that other speculators undertake in anticipation of the "Goldman roll." This involves taking sell positions on the near-dated future before the roll period (at a higher price than would be available during such period) and buy positions on the far-dated future (at a lower price than during the roll period). When these positions are closed during the roll period, speculators manage to buy short-term for less and sell long-term for more than they originally spent during the pre-roll phase, thereby making a profit.[47] The fact that a number of speculators all engage in the same activity in anticipation of the roll, however, also acts as a mechanism that further depresses near-dated futures and inflates later-dated ones,[48] thereby nudging the market towards contango and rising commodity prices even more, so as to make this kind of speculation a positive feedback force[49] that compounds the contango bias already induced by index rolls. Finally, as commodity prices keep rising, more financial operators are attracted to commodity markets. As new money pours in, the size of long-only positions by index speculators increases, so that the market's bias towards contango and rising prices is further amplified.[50]

The contango bias of commodity markets as a result of index speculation ultimately makes the possibility of de-coupling investment in commodities from externalities in the real world just a fiction. Some scholars have argued that it is logically impossible for investment in derivative instruments to cause a rise in commodity prices, starting from the assumption that these may only rise if physical commodities are actually hoarded and scarcity is artificially increased on the market.[51] However, the effect of commodity index speculation is to make the price rise *precede* the hoarding of commodities by participants with access to physical storage facilities (rather than the hoarding preceding the price hike), who will hoard supplies precisely in response to the distorted price signal (rather than the other way around).[52]

This is further exacerbated by uncertainty about the part played by index speculators at any given time, as only the latter have details on the specific size of the futures positions they will roll.[53] It is therefore difficult to know whether a price change is the result of speculation or of changes in the economic fundamentals. When price information becomes muddled, it is therefore possible that it affect the behavior of economic operators, even when movements are purely speculative.[54] It does not help that part of the toolkit of market operators and observers includes neoclassical models that systematically impute changes in price to economic fundamentals, thereby exacerbating the tendency of operators to act based on prices, as if the latter always conveyed information about the relative scarcity of a particular commodity.[55]

In sum, the dynamics affecting the markets for agricultural commodities since the year 2000 display a high degree of the self-referentiality, which—as I have argued in Chapter 2—is one of the central features of the contemporary system of global finance. Price movements feed into each other with little weight given to information about economic fundamentals. As a consequence, "food" becomes just another asset entangled in a web where everything is an investment and an opportunity to reap financial profit. When these dynamics are translated into the world of "real" economic variables, however, the effects are often deeply destabilizing, as lucidly exemplified by the 2008 world food price crisis. More generally, the volatility of markets for agricultural commodities has been sending—on a day-to-day basis—systematically wrong signals to producers, causing over-sowing or under-cultivation.[56] Finally, whereas higher commodity prices have trickled down to consumer markets, the hike of 2008 has not been followed by a symmetrical decrease (as it occurred on international commodity markets). Higher prices have "stuck," especially in countries without adequate structures in place to guarantee domestic food sufficiency and whose currencies have suffered depreciation vis-à-vis the dollar, thereby making it possible for prices of dollar-denominated imports to stay high even after the decline in global food prices after 2008.[57] This, however, is not the end of the story. Finance does not only dissolve "food" as only one in a web of financial assets open for investment, as exemplified by direct speculation on financial markets. Instead, financial motives increasingly make their way into corporate boardrooms and become one of the drivers behind novel assemblages in the production of "food" today.

5

The Finance-Driven Engineering of Food

In this chapter, I address in greater depth the "capture" of the food economy by financial motives, which was already introduced in Chapter 2. In particular, I look at how "food" is increasingly engineered following imperatives for financial profitability, that have the result of weakening relations of co-production between man and nature which lay at the heart of the peasant condition.[1] In this respect, the necessary point of departure is the changed relationship to food production which affects farmers squeezed between market forces along the food supply chain. These forces increase their dependence and reduce the room available for building a resilient, productive agricultural resource base. Following this, I turn then to analyze some of the forces that compress the options available for modern farmers, focusing in particular on the role of transnational agrifood corporations and supermarkets. The goal I hope to attain through this targeted panoramic is to highlight the limits arising from the adoption of a shared metric of financial profit across the different levels of the food supply chain, which systematically obliterates the more-than-economic logic underpinning the peasant condition, centered as it is on maintenance of and stewardship for the natural resource base.

Farming for Money

Ploeg[2] defines the peasant condition as consisting both of an element of resistance and an element of autonomy. In other words, it can be characterized as both an attempt to minimize dependency relations (e.g. from the market), as well as a practice of building autonomy through the creation of a resilient farm that relies mostly on inputs that are produced internally. The two aspects are to some extent sides of the same coin, as the building of autonomy — especially vis-à-vis market-mediated relations — carves spaces of resistance to the profitability calculus of economic relations, replacing that logic with different metrics of success endogenous to the peasant world,[3] as exemplified for instance by the concept of "beautiful farm."[4] It is within this background that the logic of farming as co-production between man and living nature acquires centrality as an ordering principle that lies outside of the logic of economic profitability that hovers over the world of food, acting both as a limit and a first victim to the expansionism of profit-driven relations under the pressure of financial imperatives.

As an alternative mode of patterning, it is the relational aspect — "co-production" — that takes primacy over the elements of "man" and "nature." Far from being fixed entities, in fact, the latter acquire their reciprocal identities precisely through the "ongoing interaction and mutual transformation"[5] entailed in the process of co-production. So, for example, in a co-production relationship "man" is moulded as a designer of ecosystems, who deploys "common sense and craft" to create a durable "habitat" to support human dwelling.[6] Similarly, "nature" receives meaning as a set of "living" relationships between different ecological components.[7] These relationships are regarded as an aid in the struggle for autonomy through the establishment of a resilient resource base, rather than an obstacle to be worked around through the superimposition of engineered connections.[8]

This relationship of co-production increasingly features as the first victim of the inclusion of farmers into market circles (which increases patterns of dependency), and the ensuing need to replace the metric of peasant quality with one based purely on cost-benefit calculations.[9] Indeed, the organic nature of agricultural productivity — which lies at the core of the logic of co-production, based as it is on the acknowledgment of and cooperation with ecological cycles — is widely recognized as an obstacle to capitalist accumulation.[10] In light of this, the inclusion of rural production within a wider web of economic relations has occurred—in a typical example of system "expansionism"—through the stripping away of ecological complexity mediated by a technological effort aimed at the simplification and standardization of agricultural production, so as to replicate the "ideal of control" experienced in the factory setting.[11] Hence, technological innovation has played a crucial role in the decline of smallholder, peasant agriculture, towards "entrepreneurial" farming based on a high dependency on markets and the ensuing internalization of the logic of financial costs and benefits.[12] It was precisely through a technification of agriculture that the latter was made less labour-intensive (thereby freeing up labour), while simultaneously retaining productivity despite increases in scale (so as to restructure agriculture as the "bread basket" of industrial centers). This technologically-driven marginalization of the peasantry has affected different parts of the world at different times: it took hold in the Western world already during the "first" food regime at the turn of the nineteenth century,[13] whereas it proceeded in several stages, but most intensely from the 1970s with the Green Revolution, in the former colonized world.[14]

Despite the wide variety in the specifics of peasant farming across the world, autonomy vis-à-vis market relations has been said to represent the edge of the struggle between peasant and more "entrepreneurial" modes of farming across the developed and the developing world.[15] In this respect, the tendency towards establishing relations of dependency with a market of mechanical and chemical inputs (such as fertilizers and pesticides) and with one of agricultural commodity outputs (dominated by agrifood corporations and retail giants),[16] has acted against the peasant principle of distancing the farm from markets to make it more resilient.[17] The squeezing of modern farming in a supply-chain-type of relation with industrial capital—both through the provision of chemical and mechanical inputs and the purchase of outputs for further processing/sale—has given rise to what has been termed the technological "treadmill."[18] In essence, as farmers increasingly move into technology-intensive, monocultural techniques, this allows them to increase their production while prices are still high. However, as more farmers do the same, prices fall, and new increases in scale and/or enhancements in technology are necessary to stay afloat. Therefore, the costs of non-farm inputs rise precisely because farmers respond to decreasing prices by increasing size and use of artificial inputs.[19] One has to add to this that, in the present day, increased concentration in the upstream sectors further compresses the prices farmers are able to obtain.[20] The result is a squeeze on farmer incomes, which has—in turn—called for state action to stabilize the conditions within which market dependency could endure without wiping out farming altogether.[21] So, for example, the European Common Agricultural Policy (CAP) is a paramount example of a scheme which was established to subsidize "industrial" agriculture, so as to hold up farmers entangled in a novel ordering that would—without these crutches—have been more fragile than peasant agriculture.[22] Within the new paradigm of "mechanized" agriculture, features like scale and specialization become key, contrary to the experience of peasant farming, where intensive (rather than extensive) cultivation and diversity rather than monocultural specialization are some of the ways in which autonomy is achieved.[23] This, of course, has occurred at the cost of forgoing the need to preserve the natural resource base, leaving unchecked a whole host of ecological problems that can be ascribed directly to technified agriculture.[24]

Additionally, the job of farming has changed drastically. It has gone from a craft-based occupation to something not much different to work on the assembly line, as farmers follow instructions to "assemble" their industrial and chemical inputs together in what has been called "farming by numbers."[25] Secondly, the need to embrace increasing technological innovation has often forced farmers into the spiral of debt.[26] Aside from making farming a frustrating, lonely experience to the point of forcing some farmers to take their own lives,[27] technification and indebtedness have also pushed aside the quality logic of peasant farming. Instead, farmers have increasingly internalized the calculative practices adopted in wider business circles, with productivity having to grow by an amount sufficient to keep up loan repayments (so that financial solvency, as opposed to ecological soundness, has become the driver of farming decisions). Ploeg[28] provides a telling example of these changing trends in relation to the choice of milking cows. When these are selected only with a view to maximize milk output given the price paid for the cow, issues such as cows' health and their breeding within the farm no longer find any space as animals become mere "throwaway inputs," which can literally be milked for a few years and then replaced with others as their productivity declines. This, of course, is possible only in a context of calculative practices that have no way of accounting for such factors as the increased resilience of using native breeds or farm-raised cows.[29]

The systematic invisibility of the peasant logic within purely economic and market relations makes it so that peasant production is regarded as a residual byproduct that will—sooner or later—be wiped away. Peasants lose, in a rural world re-patterned after market principles, their right to exist as peasants and the conditions for their enduring reproduction are curtailed through takeover of their development possibilities.[30] Takeover can take a myriad possible shapes. Some concrete examples are: forcing a market of milk quotas upon small producers (resulting in a concentration of opportunities for milk production upon entrepreneurial farms),[31] the curtailment of access to crucial resources such as water supplies in Catacaos (Peru),[32] the imposition of regulatory measures that only entrepreneurial farms are able to meet.[33] This last case is exemplified by the standardization of hygiene practices in relation to the processing of foodstuffs in the EU.[34] So, for example, EC Regulation 852/2004 lays out general requirements to which premises on which food processing takes place have to comply. The Regulation allows the competent local authorities to derogate from these general rules, in order to accommodate the needs of local, on-farm and small-scale production.[35] However, inertia at the level of local authorities in carving out exceptions has practically translated in the imposition of requirements that peasant farmers can hardly meet,[36] considering the size of own production rarely makes it worthwhile to undertake the investment needed to comply with rules put in place with the entrepreneurial farmer in mind.[37] In this respect, paradigmatic examples are the request to plaster the dry stone walls of a room where cheese is ripened,[38] as well as the possibility of exclusion of the dwelling-house from the places on which foodstuffs may be lawfully "processed" (where "processing" is understood to include heating, say for making jam or tomato puree, or the ripening of cheeses).[39]

In sum, as agriculture undergoes a re-patterning after purely economic values, the set of calculative practices centered on financial cost and benefit hijack the peasant logic of farming and simultaneously strengthen relations of dependence to financial institutions (such as banks), markets and agrifood corporations that erode the space available for peasant relations to endure. Increasingly often, this process of "monetization" translates into chronic short-termism that—from an ecological point of view— depletes the very resource base, the reproduction of which is essential to the production of food in the long run.[40] This is the clearest illustration of the phenomenon of economic expansionism which has been discussed in Chapter 2: on the one hand, the economic system needs an environment of more-than-economic relations to support itself.[41] On the other hand, the economy engages in a coercive projection of its internal code to re-pattern "virgin" spaces according to economic principles. This, in turn, prevents the ability of such extra-economic spaces to endure by reproducing themselves and by recycling the byproducts of the economic system's metabolism. In the long run, this expansionism—when it goes unchecked—poses a threat to the enduring ability of the environment to support the economic system, which in turn nudges the economy itself towards increasing entropy.

Food Multinationals

One of the defining traits of the third food regime has been the onset of transnational food corporations (TNCs), thanks to the liberalization brought about by structural adjustment programmes in the developing world and the WTO treaties, as well as by the free circulation of capital after the collapse of the Bretton Woods system. Food TNCs can best be thought of as wide-ranging networks orchestrating a range of connected processes across a diverse range of markets:[42] from supply of agro-chemicals and seeds to processing of farm output, from manufacture of consumer products to distribution and retail (this last segment of TNCs I analyze deeper in the following section).[43] Typically, food TNCs will embrace one or more of these different markets, thereby controlling different stages of the supply chain located upstream or downstream (vertical integration). Another mechanism through which such networks develop is horizontal integration, whereby competing businesses in the same sector are somehow incorporated in the TNC.[44] The result is that, through a set of arrangements, such as mergers, joint ventures and partnerships, the food supply chain is increasingly dominated by what have been called "food clusters"[45] or "food empires."[46] The oft mentioned "hourglass" shape of food supply chains, where a myriad farmers (the top of the hourglass) produce food, which then goes through the "bottleneck" of agrifood corporations prior to final delivery to a myriad of consumers, is the outcome of such concentration processes at the level of TNCs. The above, of course, is still an imperfect picture, if one considers that the impact of agribusiness can be felt even ahead of agricultural production, through—for example—the need for farmers to purchase seeds. These seeds are engineered to work with particular chemical inputs, and displace native varieties that—while less productive in a monocultural setting—are typically better adapted to local ecologies, and hence more resilient to locally adverse conditions.

The ensuing picture is one in which the conditions for undertaking food production are increasingly "fenced" and determined outside of the farm: from seeds and other inputs to the prices and even the quality specifications of agricultural outputs. In light of this, the essence of TNC networks—as an expression of the pervasive economization of the food system—lies precisely in the assertion of exclusionary control over the channels through which resources are routed. From this control comes the possibility to appropriate value that is created elsewhere. TNC networks do not work much differently from a feudal landlord levying tolls on bridges within his tenure (thereby siphoning away value that was not directly produced by the landlord himself). They exercise oversight over the assemblage of "food" while, in the meantime, levying a toll at the different stages that resources go through from farm to fork.[47] Unlike the landlord that actually owns the road on which he levies a toll, however, TNCs do not need to own a lot of physical infrastructure (e.g. a slaughterhouse or processing facility), nor do they need to generate the resources that flow across physical infrastructures (livestock in the case of the slaughterhouse, or agricultural produce in the case of the processing facility). Crucial, instead, is simply the ability of routing such flows. And TNCs are able to do so through the selective opening of market channels at targeted nodes. This induces competition to seize the "opportunit[ies] to access the connections that allow the product to be routed to areas of wealth,"[48] the availability of which is rationed by TNCs. This, in turn, gives TNCs control over the channeling of resources—now turned into "commodities"—across the vast network over which they exert their control.[49] Access to the networks administered by TNCs is crucial for—say—farmers needing to sell their produce, or for small businesses looking for outsourced production. Through relationships of dependence from a "food empire," these actors can be coerced into various sorts of conditions, relating to price, or quality, or production methods.[50] The ability to set conditions and, therefore, effectively to exert exclusionary control over the underlying flows, becomes then a source of value, an asset that can be leveraged for the purpose of generating profits.[51] This is a crucial point. As the development of finance as a self-referential system locks assets in a panopticon where resources that are not sufficiently profitable can be restructured to conform to current expectations of financial return, it is this ability to restructure and re-arrange flows of resources (rather than ownership of the resources themselves) that represents the essence of financial control, to enable the extraction of value. This has been argued to be a trend also outside of the food system. So, for example, social networks like Facebook control "assets" that are nothing more than the ability to route relationships among normal people.[52] In relation to food, this tendency is embodied in the ability of TNCs to gatekeep essential nodes in the production process. This is the passage through which various stages involved in the production of food can be made available for restructuring—thereby being treated purely as "assets"—after breaking down the relationship of co-production between man and nature in order to enforce the metrics of financial profitability. The linear rewiring of an otherwise organic process, by putting in place a set of economic connections mediating control and value extraction, can clearly be seen at work in the processes of "appropriationism" and "substitutionism" outlined in Chapter 3 (whereby agriculture is progressively wedged between industrial capitals from both the side of input and that of output).

This process is even more alive and varied today, in the context of the "capture" of industrial capital by financial imperatives. So, for example, the presence of TNCs on stock markets has enhanced the weight of shareholder value as a measurement of performance. In this context, restructurings that allow an inflation of share prices have become more frequent. A prime (but clearly not the only) expression of these being precisely the flurry of mergers and acquisitions that have affected also the world of food.[53] The process is the usual: mergers and acquisitions enable the enlargement of the network of connections to which access can be restricted, so as to enhance control over resources produced elsewhere. This heightened degree of control, in turn, translates in a higher valuation of a company's aggregate assets.[54] Furthermore, it is the anticipation of these share price increases that pushes financial institutions to provide TNCs with the funds to finance such takeovers in the first place.[55]

The shareholder link, however, is just one of the ways in which the logic and calculative practices of the financial system capture the food economy. Indeed, some textbook examples of food TNCs are actually companies that are not floated on a stock market. Cargill, for example, which is active in a wide range of markets from seed manufacture to grain trading, happens to be the largest privately owned venture in the world. This notwithstanding, even a company seemingly insulated from financial markets couples control over a network of processes relating to food production with a thriving financial arm which is not immediately related to its core business.[56] In this hybrid TNC, the food-related part of the business becomes just another kind of asset, which is managed alongside a wider portfolio of financial activities.[57] In light of this, and of a more general context where the metrics of financial profit direct corporate decision-making,[58] it is inevitable that food production comes to be regarded merely as a process that can be deconstructed and reconstructed with a view to the extraction of "latent value,"[59] even for a private company like Cargill.[60]

The best elucidation of this phenomenon, whereby food production becomes subject to financial imperatives, has been reported by Ploeg[61] in a study of Parmalat. Parmalat is an Italian-based multinational operating in the dairy sector, which went bankrupt in 2003. Parmalat was entangled in a wide financial network, and—especially towards the end—was under increasing pressure to mine value from the assets it controlled to sustain financial credibility. In this respect, it attempted to launch a new product, *latte fresco blu*, which aimed to compete on the fresh milk market (therefore potentially putting many smaller farmers out of business), without actually being "fresh milk." In fact, while typically fresh milk is milk that is sold shortly after harvesting, *latte fresco blu* was milk bought for cheap in Poland and then subject to various processes of micro-filtration that—in the end—left little nutritional value in the resulting product and caused the milk to come to the market after a considerable amount of time.[62] After successfully lobbying for making it lawful to market such a product with the label "*latte fresco* blu" (which means "blue fresh milk") Parmalat was then able to attempt to displace producers of fresh milk proper and increase its own market share. Interestingly, in this case financial pressures spurred a big TNC like Parmalat to use its control over a set of resources in order to assemble something which turned out to be in competition with actual "fresh milk." So, what can be called "food" was bent here to financial motives, presenting an unsettling picture of the lengths to which economic expansionism—bolstered by the logic of the financial system—can radically change the face of an otherwise organic process of food production. By controlling the flows of agricultural resources channelled through the food system, TNCs are able to enact a coercive re-patterning of production flows leading to the progressive artificialization of food[63] that—however—allows them (as it did in the case of *latte fresco blu*) to take advantage of global sourcing strategies. Further examples readily come to mind, such as the distribution of juice made from concentrate, which—again—allows the sourcing of cheap fruit, its transportation as concentrate and reconstitution as juice close to the place of consumption.[64] In sum, control over resource flows is what allows the mobilization of new assets.[65] Through this control it is possible to re-pattern relations across the network of food production. In an increasingly financialized food economy, this is the way in which assets (acquired through control over resource flows) are "restructured" to deliver returns comparable to those of other classes of financial assets, against which corporate performance is increasingly being measured.[66]

Big Retail

Among food TNCs, a somewhat special niche is occupied by big retail chains. While the level of vertical integration of other agrifood TNCs has been high, it has not—however—managed comprehensively to embrace all the stages of the supply chain, so as to exert farm-to-fork control over it. A substantial degree of control over production, consumption and distribution seems, however, to have been the domain of supermarket chains.[67] Thanks to a wide distribution network, supermarket chains have managed to gate-keep important connections with producers and consumers. First of all, they have increasingly started to get involved in food production, either by the setting of quality standards to be met by suppliers, or—directly—by starting own-brand product lines.[68] Secondly, the very history of the supermarket is one of control around the conditions in which consumers "meet" food products.

The setting of conditions to suppliers, as I have discussed in the previous section, is at the heart of the "imperialistic" character of food TNCs, whereby—by acting as gatekeepers of far-reaching webs of connections—they are able to extract a toll from whoever chooses (or, most often, needs) to access their networks.[69] On the other hand, by starting their own product lines, supermarkets increasingly compete with agrifood corporations traditionally involved in the middle stages of processing. In this respect, direct access to a body of consumers affords them with (1) the ability to respond quickly to changing consumer tastes, by adapting their own-brand offer and (2) to nudge consumer taste towards particular products. Curiously enough, the production of own-brand foods is often outsourced, so that supermarkets don't actually own any production facilities. Hence, their profits do not stem from possession of a physical infrastructure, or even from originating the resources that flow through it. Instead, they simply extract value from the ability to gate-keep connections to consumers. In turn, the flexibility required by manufacturers of own-brand products to meet changing demands is subsequently externalized upon workers, who end up having to pay a "toll," in terms of pay levels, working hours or job insecurity,[70] to be able to access the productive assemblage of the manufacturing company and—in turn—the outstretched network of the supermarket from which value accrues to their labour.

Consumer-retailer relations display somewhat more open dynamics than a one-way relationship between supermarkets and consumers, whereby the former respond to feedback coming from the latter. Indeed, the very history of supermarkets is couched in the ability to alter the conditions under which consumers "connect" to food products. The first "self-service" supermarket as we know it—the "Piggly Wiggly" in Memphis—was predicated on a structure whereby consumers would effectively do the shopping for themselves, so as to do away with shop clerks that would fetch products for them. Furthermore, they would go through all of the supermarket's stock before reaching the check-out.[71] Nowadays, the shopping experience is arranged in increasingly sophisticated ways that—while not requiring consumers to go through a pre-established path—actually build on "browsing" patterns increasingly monitored by information technologies.[72] Above this, the very distribution of supermarket retail arms has been dubbed "expansionist,"[73] as they "prey on the existing diversity of towns and local centres"[74] and develop large stores—often out of town—from which to enlarge their market share. In this way, they are able to "mine" into wealthier customer segments (those that have access to a car to access out-of-town stores, or live in the wealthier neighborhoods where retail chains decide to develop a presence), giving rise to "food deserts" in poorer areas. Here, access to nutritious food is curtailed because of the shutting down of alternative distribution mechanisms for fresh produce as a consequence of the super-markets' very expansion.[75] It follows that—in a food desert—available nutritional options are typically less healthy than those available elsewhere.[76] Last, but not least, supermarkets are always working at strengthening connections with consumers through various strategies, from loyalty schemes to subtler processes of authority building, e.g. as health and lifestyle authorities.[77]

Just as any TNC, control over connections through which resources flow is purely instrumental to mining value from the food chain in such a way as to sustain financial profitability. This is attained both by shuttling food across the globe to wealthy consumers—increasing "food miles"[78]—as well as by re-ordering food production so as to "add value," in a bid to follow a demand for "quality" that allows to extract price differentials from discerning customers.[79] However, the restructuring of assets can also take the shape of major overhauls, as in the case of what was formerly the Somerfield supermarket chain. In essence, Somerfield was acquired by a private equity firm that, through layoffs, streamlining of product lines and massive real estate sales (whereby it transferred them to a specially created new company, that was able to raise funds using its real estate portfolio as collateral), was able to re-arrange the web of connections controlled by the chain in such a way as to maximize its financial performance. It eventually sold Somerfield (for a profit) to the Co-operative Group, now the fifth largest food retailer in the UK.[80] Additionally, some major supermarket chains have also started expanding into consumer credit by starting their own banks:[81] which, again, can be understood as an attempt to restructure/expand control in such a way as to tap into new stores of value, further and further away from food production, so as to diversify and continue boosting the profitability of the company's asset "portfolio."

To summarize, the ways in which the financial "capture" of the real economy reverberates on the process of food production display a high degree of subtlety. In this chapter, I started from a view of peasant forms of co-production, centered on an acknowledgment of the organic nature of the rural production process. From there, I have analyzed ways in which this process is increasingly jeopardized by the encroachment of industrial and financial capital. One way is through a progressive loss of resilience on the part of farming units, increasingly squeezed between a market of industrial inputs and a concentrated front of purchasers that leaves them dependent on subsidies. I have then focused on the players encountered outside of the farm gates, which increasingly are multinational corporations. These are now entangled in a circuit of financial pressures coming either from the stock markets, or from debt exposure, or even yet from the general sharing of calculative practices centered on financial turnover and heightened profit expectations. In light of this, the central character of TNCs has been pinpointed in their ability to exert exclusionary control over the process of food production, locking out other players (e.g. farmers or outsourced manufacturers) at strategic locations by the opening of market channels from which to be able to extract a rent. Within the TNC camp, supermarkets have shown to be those best placed to obtain a comprehensive degree of oversight over the supply chain, thanks to control over the connections between consumers and the final product. Throughout this overview, it has become evident how the food production process progressively loses its organic character of co-production. It is, instead, increasingly broken up in stages that—through a new identity as assets capable of providing a remuneration for the capital expended in their takeover—are open for restructuring to match returns available from other financial assets. In this respect, it is therefore possible to speak of a "transnational space of corporate agricultural and food relations integrated by commodity circuits"[82] that increasingly restricts possibilities of relating to food in a more-than-economic way through the logic of peasant co-production. In so doing, the financialized food economy represents once again a clear example of system expansionism, whereby the environment within which economic relations are sustained is increasingly bent to the logic of the economy itself, depleting its ability to regenerate itself and thereby sustain the economic system in the long run.

6

The Case of Coffee

The dynamics at work within the set of actors and institutions involved in the production, processing and distribution of coffee—the "coffee complex"—offer a fruitful illustration of some of the issues discussed thus far, from the speculation on commodities to the exploitation of farmers by TNCs. In order to illustrate the evolution of the coffee complex, this chapter sketches a historical panorama of coffee production, contextualizing it within the food regimes approach, which has been introduced in some depth in Chapter 3. After describing the steps leading to an international coffee trade based on principles of competition among countries (the first coffee regime), the chapter introduces the second coffee regime. This was characterized by the development of an international trade framework for coffee, through the agreements between consumer and producer countries enabled within the purview of the International Coffee Organization. Simultaneously, a transformation of coffee production and consumption also took place, in the light—for example—of the introduction of Green Revolution productive technologies in developing countries, and of the development of a standardized mass market in the developed world. These historical remarks are then weaved together in the description of the current state of the coffee complex. The main features of the present situation are (1) the collapse of the framework provided by the International Coffee Organization since 1989, (2) the appearance of changing patterns of consumption, as exemplified by the rise of specialty and sustainable coffee, and (3) the "privatization" of global governance—at least as far as trade relations in the case of coffee are concerned—that has been engendered by, for example, the fair trade movement.

The First Two Coffee Regimes

As attested by its origin in Ethiopia, coffee is a plant that is most adapted to tropical and subtropical climates.[1] As a consequence, from its early success in the Islamic world, it went on to become a staple of colonial relations starting from the eighteenth century.[2] In particular, coffee production and consumption patterns reflected the well-known dynamics of colonial specialization, in which the colonies supplied raw or semi-processed commodities to the mainland,[3] so that—effectively— "[c]olonialism dictated where coffee was cultivated."[4]

The First Coffee Regime

As Latin American countries acquired independence from Spain and Portugal, an international coffee market started to develop. While the geographic pattern of coffee trade broadly followed the established colonial flows directed to the metropolitan centers,[5] the mode of regulation of such exchanges changed from colonial administration to trade relations between sovereign nations.[6] In this respect, alongside the birth of international trade in temperate commodities discussed by Friedmann and McMichael,[7] the onset of global trade relations equally affected tropical commodities such as coffee.[8] In this new scenario, a "trade war" developed—in the early decades of the twentieth century—between Brasil and Colombia, respectively the first and second largest coffee producer in the world. A fundamental role, in this "first" coffee regime, was played by national producer associations, the Instituto Brasileiro do Café (Brasilian Coffee Institute, hereinafter IBC) and the Federación National de Cafeteros (National Federation of Coffee Producers). While the former effectively acted as a marketing board and—in particular—enacted policies of managed supply (such as the hoarding and destruction of coffee from the markets to keep prices high)[9] in order to make the most of Brasil's initial monopoly,[10] the latter aggressively competed for a larger share of international trade by seeking to expand production, while free-riding on the stabilization policies of the IBC.[11]

The Second Coffee Regime

It is with the end of World War II that the coffee system entered its own "second" regime. Typically, the second food regime is equated with an increasing degree of state intervention in national agricultural policy, in order to buffer domestic production from increasing international competition. In the case of tropical commodities, national regulation of production actually sparked the need for increased international cooperation between producer countries. This, in order to confront one of the main challenges facing coffee producers, namely deteriorating trade terms.[12] In particular, after the entrance on the world market for coffee of African countries (in which coffee had been promoted aggressively by the French colonial administration[13]), the front of coffee supply became even more fragmented and unable to coordinate production. This made it increasingly evident that the costs that any single producing country had to shoulder to keep world prices high were generating external benefits to competing producers that were not withholding exports. This, in turn, enhanced the need for some form of international cooperation amongst coffee producers.[14]

It was only with the onset of the Cold War that the United States—the largest market for coffee consumption—saw the opportunity to contribute to the stabilization of world coffee prices: an effort which can be read in conjunction with the beginning of the "development project" as a new hegemonic strategy—on the part of the United States—to preserve its position in the face of the threat of Communism.[15] It is in this changed political and economic climate, therefore, that the International Coffee Organization (ICO) saw the light in 1962.[16] The ICO was—and still is—an organization uniting producer and consumer countries, which was devised as a forum to implement agreements in which market quotas were arranged between producer countries and enforced in consumer countries, with a view to manage the worldwide supply of coffee and stabilize prices.

The same climate that gave birth to the ICO also came with another important trend, which Luttinger and Dicum refer to as the "technification" of coffee,[17] meaning the promotion of Green Revolution technologies amongst producer countries (often funded through development aid). These innovations encroached on traditional coffee varieties and growing practices, which were characterized by more diversified production and — with it — the availability of alternative sources of income for small farmers.[18] The idea behind the switch was that the adoption of high-yield varieties of coffee beans, along with the specialization of production, could boost the incomes of poor smallholder farmers (which make up the majority of producers[19]) in producing countries.

Simultaneously, as the ICO kept coffee prices relatively high, further concentration occurred in the roasting sector,[20] exacerbating a tendency — the increase in size of firms involved in the coffee sector — which had been unfolding steadily since the development of a mass consumer market for coffee, with its hub in the United States.[21] The increasing concentration of the coffee supply chain at the level of roasters, coupled with the subsequent collapse of the ICO, played a crucial role in fundamentally altering the value-structure of the coffee supply chain, giving roasters the larger share of the cake.[22]

The Third Regime

Despite the price stability that it brought, the ICO was not free from serious shortcomings, which — coupled with an altered political and economic climate — eventually led to the suspension of the quota-setting function of the International Coffee Organization in 1989 (although the ICO still exists, its mission being to "strengthen the global coffee sector and promote its sustainable expansion in a market-based environment"[23]).

Changing consumer preferences for *arabica* over *robusta* (these are the two existing varieties of coffee beans) were not met by a swift adaptation of production quotas by ICO-member countries. Their rigidity, in turn, caused a tidal change in the attitude of the politically powerful roasting companies towards the price regime enacted by the ICO. This, coupled with arguments over quota breaches between producing countries,[24] which divided their own front, as well as a changed political economy of development focusing—in the 1980s—on market liberalization,[25] led to the demise of the quota-setting system that had been at work until then.

Market Liberalization

The ensuing liberalization of the market for coffee, in which ICO-member and non-member countries now sell their produce on an equal footing, has led to a predictable collapse in prices. Here is when many of the factors that had been at work in the previous regimes finally play themselves out in structuring the contemporary coffee complex.

The disappearance of a powerful coalition of producing countries has eliminated any buffer between a fragmented supply and a highly concentrated segment of roasters (with four companies—Nestlé, Philip Morris-Kraft Foods, Procter & Gamble and Sara Lee/Douwe Egberts—estimated to hold a 45% share of the global market for coffee[26]). This has tipped the power balance along the coffee supply chain. In addition to that, a changed international economic order—as embodied in the World Trade Organization—may stand in the way of renewed attempts to revamp quota-setting systems by virtue of their potential for distorting market mechanisms.[27]

Furthermore, the development strategies embodied in the Washington Consensus during the 1980s and implemented through vigorous Structural Adjustment Programs[28] led both to a demise of any structures capable of exerting control on supply—marketing boards—even if only domestically, and to the implementation of policies supporting the production of export commodities (such as coffee).[29] Along with the rapid rise of new producing countries like Vietnam,[30] this has led to a flooding of the international coffee market, lowering the prices producing farmers are able to receive. The default response on the part of the latter is typically to increase individual production. Their goal here is to preserve incomes by selling more at a lower price—a reaction also caused by the lack of rural diversification caused by the "technification" of coffee during the second regime. As a consequence, the predicament of producing farmers in the global coffee value chain is now clearly dismal.[31]

Commodity Speculation

Additionally, the (liberalized) coffee market presently appears to be not only one of falling, but also of highly volatile prices.[32] After the collapse of the ICO's role in global price setting, price volatility came to be hedged on futures markets.[33] As seen in Chapter 4, since futures allow one to hedge against price fluctuations, it can then appear odd that a free commodity market ought to be less stable than a regulated one, as it instead appears to be.[34] However, as shown at length in Chapter 4, speculation brings about instability on commodity markets. This is because a significant amount of trading occurs regardless of the intention to seize physical possession of the underlying asset.[35] It follows that the speculative trading of futures, de-coupled from underlying "real" variables, makes it harder for markets to process information about fundamentals and, therefore, increases volatility.[36] This is also true in the coffee market.[37]

It is not just "pure" speculators that make money from coffee price fluctuations. Increasingly, even commercial coffee traders have expanded their financial involvement beyond the immediate scope of their core business.[38] This lends support to the idea discussed in earlier chapters, that processes along the food supply chain are increasingly becoming relevant as mere assets inside wider portfolios, within which their profitability is commensurated to that of other, heterogeneous classes of assets. Going back to the case of coffee, the above shows how actors on the more concentrated side of the market appear to manage, and even to thrive in an environment of volatile prices. On the other hand, increased volatility and price bubbles trickle down to the farmers producing coffee, whose contracts are often indexed to futures prices, without them having access to hedging instruments. Farmers are, therefore, the weak link which has to surf the wave of commodity prices and translate it into decisions about how much or how little to plant, despite it not providing reliable information on levels of supply or demand on the market.[39] These difficulties compound existing disparities along the supply chain, by potentially making farmers willing to accept even lower prices in order to stabilize their incomes.[40]

New Directions in Retail

If the international coffee market therefore appears to be "controlled by the hedging and speculative strategies of transnational trading corporations on the futures and spot markets,"[41] the massification of consumption of the second food regime appears to have given rise to new competitive strategies—on the retail side—in the form of "global sourcing [...], product differentiation [...] and product innovation.[42] These strategies, as observed more generally in Chapter 5, allow agrifood companies to "mine" additional value from an otherwise saturated market. So, the retail sector is still dominated by large roasting companies that source coffee internationally based on price signals. These have also diversified their products through the introduction of—for example—instant coffee (which makes up the vast majority of coffee consumption in some markets, like the UK) or decaf coffee,[43] as well as coffee-based soft drinks,[44] in an attempt to halt the decline in coffee consumption that had otherwise been taking place since the 1970s.[45]

The Specialty Coffee Segment and Fair Trade

However, the most interesting new trends seem to have come in the form of specialty coffees and, building on the rise of the latter, sustainable coffee.[46] The former simply refers to the valuation of a coffee's "origin, quality, processing and cultivation methods"[47] as a significant contributor to the product's taste. Specialty coffee has been another way—for large retailers—to tap into a different type of demand.[48] The best example of this strategy is perhaps Nestlé's "Nespresso" business model, which generates consumer fidelity by coupling household coffee-making technology with a variety of flavours—seeking to accommodate a gourmet clientele—packed in pre-fit capsules that yield a consistent quality coffee for home consumption.[49] However, specialty coffee has also fostered the expansion of large coffee "boutique" shops, where the dark drink is only part of the offer, the rest being the availability of a "non-home, non-work environment that had once been the forum for public life but that had almost disappeared under the postwar regime of highly regimented schedules, commuter life, and television."[50] Retailers like Starbucks and, later, Costa Coffee and Caffé Nero, are the clearest examples of this new trend.

Building on the differentiation introduced by the specialty coffee industry, consumer choice has been claiming attention for reasons beyond just taste, focusing instead on other concerns such as environmental sustainability/biodiversity (as is the case of organic coffee or shade-grown coffee[51]). An exemplary instance of this "wider choice" trend is the Fair Trade movement, based on the philosophy of "shortening" the supply chain, enabling direct contact between consumers and producers.[52] In view of this, Fair Trade has enabled concerns for the welfare of coffee growers to trickle down the food chain,[53] engendering what has been called the "privatization of foreign policy,"[54] i.e. the harnessing of private international trade relations for the pursuit of broadly socio-economic goals. Fair Trade has been promoted through the use of third-party certification, a form of private regulation that is now ubiquitous in the food system more generally, attesting, in particular, to the presence of those product attributes which are considered to be relevant to consumers.[55] What the coffee complex illustrates well, however, is the extent to which attention to the broader socio-economic costs of coffee has led to a competition in private standards, seeking to co-opt alternatives inside the existing system. So, for example, major brands have also tried to produce their own certification schemes outside of the more recognized Fair Trade network (centered around the Fairtrade Labelling Organizations International), attempting to ride the sustainability wave without significant changes to their business model.[56] More generally, while recognized as a positive development, the Fair Trade initiative has also been ascribed with several limits that stand in the way of its effort to bring justice to the coffee supply chain. For instance, fair trade products typically cost more than non-fair trade ones, making it a chiefly upscale phenomenon[57] pegged on a demand for higher quality[58] that inevitably excludes some farmers. Furthermore, it is uncertain to what extent fair-trade can change some of the TNCs (which include large retail chains) that are the primary cause of the squeeze on farmer incomes. In particular, it appears difficult to set conditions on them for stocking fair trade products, because of the need to use their networks to broadcast the fair trade message in the first place.[59]

In conclusion, it seems like the accumulation of capital—in relation to the coffee complex—has acquired ever more pervasive forms over time. Building on the birth of an international market and the collapse of the ICO's quota-setting system, it appears like the third "coffee regime" is characterized by the increasing tendency to devise and exploit new opportunities for profit-making. This is exemplified, for example, by the increasing differentiation of products available on the mass market (so as to create new "niches" of value from which profits may be extracted) which—particularly as concerns the mass consumption of supermarket coffee—can often be simply a matter of brand differentiation, rather than actual product improvement.[60] Similarly, the growth of specialty coffee-houses has also led to a commodification of "community," profiting on the provision of public spaces that had been lost over time, albeit doing so at the expense of actual independent coffee houses that have been outcompeted by businesses like Starbucks.[61] Specialty coffee also represents a successful attempt to exploit attempts at individual differentiation[62] through the provision of "lifestyle signifiers."[63] Finally, the liberalization of the international coffee market has afforded additional opportunities for the generation of profit simply by speculation—thereby bypassing the need to transform capital into goods for it to be possible to reap a profit. This, of course, has typically occurred at the expense of any stability in the markets concerned, creating additional problems for those that are involved in the business of producing actual commodities.[64]

In this horizon, the growth of alternative food networks along the lines of the Fair Trade movement represents a grassroots response that tries to blend the logic of enterprise with that of "connectivity,"[65] following a pattern of re-embedding of economic activity in relation to social and environmental concerns, which has been documented in literature on globalization more generally.[66] Of course, similar responses to global problems are by no means straightforward in the shape they take, and may actually entail a large degree of conflict among different players with different interests, as in the case of independent versus business codes of conduct for "fair trade" coffee.

In sum, it appears that the story of the coffee complex is polarized between an increasing diversification in the modes of capital accumulation under the profit-making motive and attempts to transform consumption of the dark drink into an occasion for renewed activism and the promotion of "other values." As such, it offers a telling exemplification of the third "food regime" described in Chapter 3. Namely, the increasingly flexible and aggressive reach of capital leads to an encroachment of more-than-economic concerns involved in the production of food (e.g. ecosystem preservation, farmer livelihoods). This movement, in turn, sparks a simultaneous globalization of struggles through the building of alternative food networks.[67]

7

Land Grabs

From the discussion carried out in earlier chapters, the "financialized" food system has emerged as a fragile Leviathan that holds together, at the cost of an increasingly aggressive outlook on the more-than-economic relations regulating the co-production of man and nature. This strain emerges, for example, from increasing instability of world food prices—a symptom of the disappearance of food as nourishment from the economic radar. Another symptom is the increasing technification of agriculture, entailing dependence on fossil fuels and simultaneously leading to a degradation in the quality of the soil. It is, in other words, a system engaged in the comprehensive displacement of organic patterns of co-production. The first step of this process is to reduce the set of relations making up the food system to just another exercise in commodity production.[1] In turn, this leads to a re-structuring of one of the fundamental bonds through which life is sustained—the co-production of nourishment from nature—after the sole metric of financial profit.

The aggressive expansionism of financial metrics of efficiency against the logic of peasant production emerges most clearly in relation to the phenomenon of land grabbing. Land grabbing is simply the large-scale acquisition of farmland in various areas of the developing world, from Africa to Ukraine. The drivers behind it are—to a large extent—a consequence of the comprehensive economization of the food system as described in earlier chapters: (1) the 2007-2008 world food price crisis, which has sparked many governments to make provisions for a world of increasingly volatile food prices;[2] (2) an increase in the demand for biofuels, due to the progressive depletion of fossil fuel availability[3] and (3) the uncertainty connected to climate change,[4] to which "technified" agriculture has been a decisive contributor.[5] As part of the "positive feedback" loop currently affecting the relationship between the economic system under the grip of financial pressures and its extra-economic environment, these symptoms have led to an ever more aggressive disciplining of the latter, under the guise of a further squeeze on agriculture. The best example of this comes precisely in the form of land grabs. Here, in fact, is where the re-patterning of co-production after economic motives turns to the basic element of agricultural production—the land—and isolates it, with a view to include it in different assemblages from which the enduring extraction of financial profit can be sustained.[6] This can go as far as acquisition of land purely with a view to benefit from price increases, explicitly treating it as just another financial asset[7] for which strong demand is foreseen (due to degradation of the planet's resources) and which can provide shelter against inflation.[8] In this chapter, I look at land grabbing, and the ways in which it is being supported by a rhetoric of development. This I do in different steps: the first section reviews the place of "agro-investor-driven" growth in the policy framework of the main development agencies. The second section then looks at the practice of agro-investment in several countries—namely India and Mozambique—particularly as it relates to the cultivation of jatropha, a plant used for biofuel production. Finally, I conclude by engaging critically with the phenomenon of large-scale acquisition of land, in light of the elements presented in the other sections.

Land Grabs and the Development Project

"Land grabs" are nothing but large-scale acquisitions of farmland by foreign investors (be they private companies or foreign governments through sovereign funds) in the developing world and—to a large extent—in Sub-Saharian Africa.[9] As a development strategy, they enhance a country's economic performance in terms of attracting "foreign direct investment."[10] In view of this, they relate to a broader evolution of agriculture in development policy, and actually constitute a revival of the idea—dating back at least to the Green Revolution—that agriculture ought to be "modernized" if development is to be attained.[11]

Land Grabs and Agrarian Development Strategies

The role of agriculture in the development project has often been subordinate to other goals such as, for example, the achievement of rapid industrialization, with respect to which it was chiefly understood to be a source of inputs and spare labour. So, for example, during the period going roughly from the end of the Second World War to the 1980s, farmers were supported to ensure they would act as a "bread basket" to back urban industrialization, or as a source of foreign currency by exporting.[12] Support for agriculture, in other words, was forthcoming only to the extent the latter could further the import-substitution policies that lay at the heart of (Keynesian) development economics, which represented the mainstream approach of the time.[13] While this came with some protection from agricultural imports, the benefits were hardly reaped by farmers, squeezed between landlord exploitation and the progressive erosion of community relations, which were giving way to market-mediated interaction.[14] Another notable occurrence in this phase was the progressive industrialization of agriculture, at least in some areas of the developing world (mostly Asia and Latin America), as well as its integration with the biotechnology complex through the introduction of "green revolution" technologies (such as high-yield seed varieties).[15] Such policies, aimed at increasing agricultural output, followed the arguments of economist W. Arthur Lewis,[16] who saw people employed in subsistence agriculture as a possible driving force for the modernization of the economy, by shifting labour from a low-productivity (if measured in financial terms) traditional sector to industries; a shift enabled precisely by the increased productivity of technified agriculture.

As Keynesian development economics eclipsed during the 1980s to be replaced by what has since come to be known as the neoliberal consensus, the subordinate role of agriculture has become perhaps even more accentuated. Indeed, it was turned into just another productive sector, under the conviction that agriculture is a business like any other and—therefore—farmers should respond to market price signals by readily shifting their offer to accommodate a matching demand.[17] This translated, for example, in the removal of any trade barriers in the form of export controls (the dismantlement of national marketing boards is a paramount example of this policy prescription). However, these measures typically led to a flooding of international markets with commodities, the price of which kept falling as farmers struggled to increase production (with falling prices) to stabilize their incomes.[18] Simultaneously, the food sufficiency of developing countries was irreversibly struck, as the latter were both spurred to convert to the production of crops for export (the fate of which on international markets has just been described) and to depend on food aid and imports from developed countries, which were seeking new markets on which to dump their agricultural surpluses.[19]

Land Grabs as Foreign Direct Investment

Now, under the pull of a financialized food economy, the need to increase the productivity of "idle" lands in the developing world has acquired new momentum. The latest assault on "virgin" spaces—to be streamlined into a novel assemblage subservient to the logic of a profit-oriented economy—embodied in the large scale acquisition of land has often been cloaked under the need to boost foreign direct investment, as a way actually to bring prosperity to the developing world. The above has led to some flagrant contradictions, as embodied in a document authored by World Bank staff, in which smallholder agricultural productivity is seen as an area of intervention through increased agricultural technology.[20] This, notwithstanding the fact that increased technification of agriculture, by increasing dependence from market relations, actually works against peasant production.[21]

The argument for stimulating foreign direct investment in developing countries traces back to the idea that—because of a lack of domestic savings—investment from abroad is crucial to set developing countries on a stable growth path.[22] Under the neoliberal paradigm, foreign investment has retained an important position, though it was no longer to be provided *directly* through foreign aid. Instead, the various reforms enacted under the guidance of the international financial institutions all aimed at generating a favourable business environment to promote (indirectly) investment from abroad (the best example of which is perhaps afforded by the Jamaican "free zones" promoted through conditional lending from international institutions[23]).

To a significant extent, the argument about the necessity of foreign investment for promoting development is still very much at play in relation to the current large scale acquisition of farmland. Indeed, according to Matondi and others,[24] this "agro-exporter model" falls squarely in the "neoliberal logic of market-based development, privatization and the transformation of natural resources," a model which is expected to "lead to maximization of investors' profits, an increase in land-based export production and the modernization of agriculture."

The tight coupling between development discourse and large-scale investment in farmland is apparent in the adoption of agro-investor-driven "development" as a justification for governmental expropriation of peasant land, with a view to make it available for foreign investment.[25] It is also evident in the backing that such practice receives from development institutions like the World Bank.[26] However, far from a naïf conviction that foreign direct investment *per se* will bring about positive changes, the World Bank has itself shown to be attuned to the dangers coming from an unregulated inflow of foreign capital. If, on the one hand, "better access to technology and markets [...] could have big poverty impacts,"[27] it is also true—on the other hand—that wholesale acquisition of farmland by foreign governments as well as foreign corporations could yield a number of negative effects, such as displacement of peasant communities, negative environmental impact and the appropriation of more land than is actually sold.[28]

In view of this, the World Bank has qualified its backing to the current wave of land acquisition through the formulation—along with other development agencies—of (voluntary) Principles for Responsible Agricultural Investment,[29] ensuring on the part of investors—for example—the acknowledgment and compliance with existing rights to land, transparency and consultation of all involved stakeholders, as well as an assessment of possible negative externalities in terms of food security, social and distributional impacts and environmental depletion. The examples illustrated in the next section, however, provide a less prosperous picture disclosed by land grabbing than is envisaged by the optimistic assessments of the World Bank.

The Case of Jatropha

Jatropha is a plant which is used in the production of biofuel. It is often presented as a win-win opportunity for local communities and international investors. This attitude is typically justified through the claim that it can be grown on marginal land and is therefore not in competition with food crops (which overcomes one of the main objections to biofuels).[30] On the hype of this "miraculous" property, jatropha has become a large source of investment in farmland in developing countries. More realistically, however, although the plant can survive in difficult conditions, this does not mean that yields will be high,[31] so that the controversy about displacement of food production is still very much alive. Furthermore, the subtraction of land for the purpose of jatropha cultivation provides a very clear example of the type of assemblage which land comes to be entangled in. In this context, in fact, land uses are determined by the most profitable process which land can be an input to,[32] regardless of questions of food sufficiency or local resilience. Which is why this section focuses explicitly on a non-food use of land to show precisely the impact of land grabs in taking the latter outside of the food system altogether (including as village commons, for example). The case studies considered in this section relate, in particular, to India and Mozambique, two countries that have jumped on the "bandwagon" of biodiesel production.

Jatropha Cultivation in Mozambique & India
Mozambique is a country in which the majority of cultivated land is entrusted to smallholder farmers, most of whom produce chiefly for their own consumption.[33] The way land tenure is regulated in Mozambique is through public ownership, on top of which a Right to Use and Develop the Land[34] is granted by the government. A crucial role in this process is played by community leaders. Predictably, some reports outline how the policy of some companies has simply been to "get the chief on board," by exerting pressure on the latter to promote and facilitate land transfer. This, it seems, is typically accompanied by a range of promises,[35] the enforceability of which—however—is often unclear, as these may not be formalized in official documents certifying the transaction.[36]

Secondly, the urge of many African governments to open their doors to agro-investment has led them to a competition in providing the most favourable business environment.[37] So, for example, in Mozambique this has resulted in the adoption of controversial policies, particularly as relates to land delimitation, transforming the latter from an automatic to a government-controlled procedure.[38] The reason this is an advantage to private investors is that, as the World Bank report by Deininger and others[39] suggests, the "encroachment on areas not transferred to the investor to make a poorly performing project economically viable" becomes harder when community areas have clear boundaries. As the delimitation of boundaries is made less transparent for communities, it becomes easier for foreign investors arbitrarily to claim that a particular plot of land has been entrusted to them. This is especially useful in relation to jatropha cultivation, since—given the lack of in-depth knowledge about the dynamics of large-scale cultivation in relation to this relatively new crop—it is not uncommon for companies to encounter difficulties in recouping their investments and breaking even.[40]

Last, but not least, even when jatropha cultivation has been undertaken by individual smallholders in the attempt to sell it on the biofuels market (so without technically requiring a "land grab"), it has still managed—despite the initial hype—to displace food production, since it has not been relegated to marginal land, and has therefore been planted in the stead of edible crops, thereby exacerbating existing problems of food sufficiency.[41]

The Indian government has also been promoting jatropha cultivation since 2003,[42] to the point of turning India into the single largest jatropha cultivator in the world.[43] The dynamics of land acquisition in India have been slightly different than they have, for example, in Mozambique, where they involved the acquisition of large expands of arable land. In India, instead, the "grab" has concerned areas that had been classified as "wasteland."[44] However, classification as "wasteland" has not occurred without controversy. Following familiar dynamics, what is considered "wasteland" for the purpose of jatropha cultivation is often land that is a valuable asset to a particular peasant community, for example as a village commons,[45] which therefore plays a role in the reproduction of that community. Additionally, Baka[46] reports how, in securing possession of the land, the companies involved have often resorted to opaque practices, resulting in the acquisition of more land than was originally agreed with the original owner. Furthermore, the resulting increase in land prices because of the "land rush" in areas selected for jatropha cultivation has effectively outpriced small farmers from the market for land.[47] Jatropha cultivation is but one example of the diversion of agricultural land to non-food uses. Recent work by Levien[48] also shows how India's experiment with Special Economic Zones has given birth to a further pathway for the subtraction of land and the displacement of the peasantry, as local governments expropriate peasant land and resell it for industrial/tertiary development. This, much like jatropha production, is a further illustration of the tendency for land to be re-arranged in new assemblages, the function of which is dictated by the most profitable options, rather than considerations of local resilience or food security. As a consequence, little consideration is given to the repercussion for the environment of more-than-economic relations that govern the cycles of co-production in peasant communities.

The Shadow of Neo-colonialism

These examples illustrate how the acquisition of land to install large-scale monocultures (or for non-agricultural purposes altogether) seems to have often taken place in a manner antagonistic to the needs of the affected communities and smallholders. In this respect, the World Bank's Principles for Responsible Agricultural Investment hardly provide any incentive to alter current practices. Indeed, as observed by the UN Special Rapporteur on the Right to Food—Olivier de Schutter—the Principles merely provide a "checklist" for interested businesses and foreign governments to engage in a large-scale acquisition of land in a way that manages to "destroy the global peasantry responsibly."[49] In fact, the Principles leave at least three interrelated sets of questions unsolved:

1 large scale investment in farmland, even when compliant with principles on responsible investment, may not be the most desirable option for agricultural development. However, under the approach of the Principles, the trade-off between a "land grab" and possible alternatives is not allowed. The comparison is simply between large-scale investment and no investment at all;[50]

2 even if large-scale investment in farmland were the most desirable option, would it still outweigh any risks stemming from its implementation? This question, in particular, ought to be considered on the background of (1) an ongoing regulatory race to the bottom by FDI-starved countries, (2) weak institutional capacity on the part of host countries for managing the complex ramifications that might be engendered by agro-investments, as well as (3) the constraints to meaningful state intervention in the regulation of investment, stemming from pre-existing bi- or multi-lateral investment agreements. According to De Schutter, "taken together, these obstacles appear insurmountable."[51]

3 Finally, the acknowledgment and compliance with land rights on the part of interested investors—as stated in the Principles—has to be read in conjunction with the World Bank's long-standing efforts to promote the formalization of property rights over land, as a way to facilitate the latter's transfer.[52] However, that assignment of individual rights of property benefits farming communities is not so straightforward as, for example, it may favour individual pressuring on the part of large investors to get the land at low prices—as reported by Baka[53] in the

case of Tamil Nadu in India—as well as making it harder to "preserve communal forms of land management."[54]

De Schutter's skepticism for the existing support for large-scale land acquisitions on the part of development institutions like the World Bank provides the basis on which to build more wide-ranging critiques of development discourse, as used in connection to "land grabbing." So, for example, it has been argued that placing emphasis on foreign direct investment as an unconditional good, as if "a load of guys who for whatever reason want to invest"[55] ought to be welcomed regardless precisely of what their reasons for investing are, represents a " 'Big Brother' attitude" resembling that of colonial times.[56]

McMichael[57] argues along similar lines. In particular, he observes how what might be occurring through the land grabs is a "rational planning of the planet"[58] to ensure the ongoing viability of an economic system otherwise lost in a runaway spiral of growth against the ecological limits of the planet.[59] In this respect, the need for agricultural modernization as a stepping stone to development is degraded as simple rhetoric,[60] hiding the building of extractive relations that resemble those of colonial times. This impression is reinforced by the fact that some of the land acquisitions are being carried out by other sovereign states, with a view to secure for themselves stable food supplies, replicating a situation typical of colonial times, namely the top-down allocation of world production following "mercantilist" goals, as opposed to production for a world market.[61] In view of this, the guidelines drafted by the World Bank become nothing more than window dressing.

The practice of large-scale acquisition of farmland in developing countries is occurring in response to a combined set of interlocked pressures, such as the world food price crisis, global warming and climate change, and increased demand for biofuels. As a result, agriculture has acquired new centrality in the development agenda. In this changed context, institutions such as the World Bank have shown support for large-scale agrarian investment, mostly on the account that it may lead to positive spillovers in terms of infrastructure, employment and foreign exchange. They have nonetheless been awake to some of the dangers inherent in unregulated capital flows, which may lend themselves to predatory dynamics vis-à-vis the peasant population of interested countries. As a consequence, the World Bank has promoted Principles for Responsible Agrarian Investment that—though voluntary—may provide a checklist of best practices to be adopted by companies wishing to invest in land.

The examples discussed in this chapter, however, undermine official optimism, and disclose instead a scenario where access to land is restricted (through the opening of a "market" for foreign investment) and subsequently re-articulated in new assemblages (e.g. biofuel cultivations) with a view to maximizing the financial (which may well be at odds with ecological) throughput of the land-based production process. Under the current conditions, the land rush appears therefore as the last stage of a spectacular global project based on the imposition of extractive relationships on the environment of more-than-economic relations that consists of peasant realities, with a view to sustain the growth of an economic system that is otherwise running against ecological limits.

8

Conclusion and Ways Forward

Hungry Capital

The food system is the set of relations governing the production of food. In traditional peasant agriculture, the food system includes feedback relations between different actors—human and natural—which work together to co-produce nourishment and a habitat for man, while enabling the continuous reproduction of the pattern of "living" relations that make up the natural ecosystem.

The economic system, on the other hand, is a pattern of relations primed to address the problem of scarcity by enacting proprietary divisions through a monetary metric. In recent years, and more strongly since the 1980s, new patterns of connectivity have branched out of the chains of payments that shape communication within the economic system, and they have instead "coiled up" into a system of their own. These new patterns, in particular, have forgone the passage of ownership of things, and developed a self-referential character, whereby financial flows build on other financial flows. In this context, owning things is no longer the prime focus of economic activity. Instead, what matters is only the ability to reap a profit from fluctuations in their monetary value. This form of "limited" ownership that does not extend to actual resources, but simply focuses on their price fluctuations, sits at the core of the phenomenon of "financialization." In a "financialized" economy, two important forces drive the economy forward: (1) the creation of new assets and (2) the ability to restructure such assets in such a way as to affect their monetary value, as a way to disclose further financial flows. This can happen in many ways. For example, "assets" can be used as collateral to obtain loans, or their value can justify

93

dividend payments to shareholders, or gains from a derivative transaction. The sort of control that matters, in other words, lies purely in the ability to organize relations between economic entities in such a way as to generate a movement in monetary values; as a result, these relations no longer matter primarily for their ability to generate this or that end product, but simply for their financial significance.

It is this feature of financial capital, i.e. its being locked in a chain of self-reference, that gives rise to what I would call "hungry capital." In the financialized economy, in fact, the reproduction of capital is less dependent on ownership of particular means of production and their assemblage into a profit-making whole, so that capital goes through cycles of "immobilization" into physical ownership and re-mobilization at the end of a productive cycle. Instead, there is an increasing attempt to restructure productive relations in such a way as to maximize their financial worth, for the immediate unlocking of "latent" value, to be monetized on financial circles through various means. It is precisely this drive to "unlock" value in financial terms that gives to the economic system its present character of an expansive, "hungry" force, attempting to re-order more-than-economic relations into strictly economic assemblages that are subject to a financial metric. In this sytem, a heightened competition between different categories of assets also arises, as the specific character of the relations packaged into an asset matters less than its financial value, and the ability to restructure them to maximize profit.

These considerations resonate with—and perhaps clarify the origin of—other common critiques of the current economic system. While these lie outside of the scope of this book, it is nonetheless useful to trace connections to enlarge the picture painted here. For example, there is mounting awareness that the practice of accounting for economic performance in terms of GDP growth is a key contributor to the depletion of the environment on which the economy relies. This practice is buttressed by key pieces of intellectual equipment, such as the description of the economy as a circular flow between families, markets and firms.[1] This hides the relationships that the economic system entertains with an environment of more-than-economic relations from which it draws resources for its continued functioning. As a result, the economy is too simplistically understood as a closed loop that can just keep cycling more and more, with little attention being paid to the structures it depletes. Against this background, conceptions of the individual as a selfish and virtually insatiable consumption machine are able flourish, and—in the process—obliterate alternative ways to assert individuality that do not involve consumption,[2] privileging ownership over relationship.[3]

Delving further into the human costs of the economy's tendency to re-arrange non-economic relationships in ways that fit its "code," one also encounters the debate on the racial and gender biases of the current economic system. So, for example, in her history of women in the transition to capitalism, Silvia Federici finds how—beyond extrapolating rural labour away from an organic unity of production and consumption, to include it as an input in industrial production[4]—the expansionism of economic relations has pressed against gender categories. In this process, women have been pushed to take on the role of "housewifes" to nurture the working class, sowing the seeds of a subalternity that endures to this day.[5] The "invisibilization" of women's work has equally occurred in agriculture: as the family farm becomes more specialized, women are relegated to complementary, gap-filling roles, that are necessary to enable the farm's reproduction.[6] As far as racial categories are concerned, the projection of attributes of backwardness upon indigenous peoples equally enabled the imposition of new productive and colonial relationships upon societies that were organized in fundamentally different ways.[7] A demonization that, far from being confined to the colonial period proper, is very much in vogue still today, cloaked under the rhetoric of expansion of the "rule of law."[8] Much, of course, is to be learnt from such related debates, of which these brief annotations offer only a flavour.

To return to food, the expansionism of the economic system under the pressure of the financial system increasingly translates into the dismembering of organic cycles of production, as embodied in peasant co-production, into linear input-output chains subject to the metric of financial profit. Farm production is increasingly dependent on external inputs (e.g. chemical fertilizers, pesticides, hybrid or genetically modified seeds, mechanical implements such as tractors) and on external output markets for agricultural commodities. When it is not outright displaced by the re-articulation of land into new assemblages which may or may not serve to produce food (e.g. biofuel production in the "land grab"). In this new environment, transnational corporations both in the processing and the retail sector increasingly have the ability to exert control over the food chain, and enact new orderings that are streamlined for the extraction of financial value. From Parmalat's attempt at re-engineering fresh milk in such a way as to maximize profit and control a larger market share to Somerfield's (fictional) transfer of its assets to itself, so as to unlock the latent value of its real estate and originate new financial flows.

Now, of course, every system is embedded in a set of relations that encompass more than the system's sectorial logic can accommodate. Co-production between man and nature embodies exactly this multi-dimensional aspect, which—however—is increasingly dismembered and swallowed up by an expanding economic system. The depletion of this extra-economic environment ultimately works against the long-term maintenance of the economic system itself, as it is less able to rely on an environment that provides it with resources and recycles its byproducts. Therefore, as this proceeds, the "financialized" economy runs against the grain of entropy, whereby—in a closed system—disorder increases leading to the unravelling of that system. In view of the foregoing, then, one burning question has to be answered. How to avert this?

Taming Hunger

Following the description above, the problem faced by the food system appears to be one of economic expansionism, whereby a particular system—the economic one—shuts down alternative patterns of relating, from which it nonetheless depends for its continuing viability. However, systems problems can be approached in a variety of ways and—in this last section—I aim briefly to discuss a few possible strategies. Indeed, despite the unsettling picture the foregoing chapters present, I do not actually believe that all is lost. Systems do possess "leverage points," from which it becomes possible to act on them in order to achieve sustainable equilibria in their interactions with the extra-systemic environment.[9]

If the addictive "hunger" of the economic system comes from its internal configuration, of course, "healing" can only come from acting on the self-organization of the system by promoting endogenous change that will make the system more resilient and less dissipative. As I have shown in Chapter 2, systems are perhaps best thought of as the products of a set of interlocking agencies acting on open-ended and partial scripts.[10] In this respect, while they may seem "hard," immutable structures, systems are instead "soft" assemblages that are constantly re-enacted by unstable agencies. In this respect, they may give rise to "disjunctures,"[11] within which new patterns can be nourished.

At every stage in the reproductive cycle of a system, in other words, there arises the possibility to nudge it towards different forms of self-organization and—therefore—different outcomes. This is, for example, the type of intervention advocated by

Teubner,[12] when he advances the idea of "capillary constitution-alism." In a very broad sense, this involves facilitating the emergence of an equilibrium between each social system and its extra-systemic environment, such that the former's reproduction does not threaten the latter's existence.[13] These equilibria can emerge when "constitutive" limits to the system's expansionism come to be inscribed in the latter's internal configuration (hence the word "constitutionalism," used in a somewhat broad sense).

This process clearly requires pressure coming from outside the economic system. So, for example, one should not underestimate the advocacy work carried out by non-governmental or intergovernmental organizations that, at various levels, attempt to bring about changes in the legal regulation of economic relations affecting the food system on a global or a national scale.[14] Notable examples are the advocacy for a better regulation of land uses, particularly with a view to limit the scope for land grabbing, carried out both by NGOs as well as the office of the UN Special Rapporteur on the Right to Food. In a report to the UN General Assembly, for example, the latter has illustrated how key human rights obligations may apply to foreign investment in farmland, thereby setting legal boundaries. The legal boundaries so proposed would in turn be open to scrutiny by existing human rights monitoring bodies.[15] Simultaneously, he has set out minimum principles that should safeguard that these boundaries are not overstepped. Among the suggested "checks" is, for example, the promotion of intensive, labour-rich agriculture,[16] the adoption of sustainable cultivation methods that integrate into the local ecology, build soil fertility and mitigate climate change,[17] as well as enhanced protection of indigenous peoples and local communities from forced evictions, also through the recognition of community (rather than individual) rights to land.[18] These principles readily appear to have at heart the preservation of peasant co-production, and can therefore represent a shield against unregulated agro-investment. On a different—yet related—note, the UN Special Rapporteur on the Right to Food has also argued for better regulation of commodity markets, so as to address some of the issues outlined in Chapters 4 and 6.[19] A different example of regulatory advocacy taking place at the national—rather than international—level is the Campaign to Protect Rural England, whose policy proposals stress the need for national and local government to engage in preserving local food webs. This involves, for example, proactive planning to preserve town centres from being drained by the spread of big retail.[20] As town centres typically house small, independent retailers such as butchers or bakers, that tend to source locally and from small farmers, this strategy would then help support a diverse ecology of small rural producers.

Beyond outside pressure from the regulatory side, however, it is ultimately essential that "endogenous growth imperatives [...] be combated with endogenous growth inhibitors,"[21] since regulation or other forms of social influence only work when they lead to a "self-domestication" of the system's growth dynamic. In this respect, forms of politicization of the consumer that operate directly on the flow of money within the economy represent an interesting possibility as they may ignite "learning adaptation."[22]

The need to "rewire" an expansionist social system appears to have been equally contemplated by Long,[23] who uses the term "counterwork." Counterwork is understood precisely as the deployment of agency within a system, in such a way as to challenge existing patterns and instead experiment with new ones,[24] so as to re-embed the system in the context of broader concerns for the continuing viability of its environment. In this respect, where the economic system closes lines of development for peasant co-production, new ones can be reinstated through different connections, so that access to consumers or financing which has been "the object of disassembling (in order to be assembled anew in accordance with the ordering principle of

Empire) is actively reconnected and re-patterned by peasants."[25] In this way, undesirable patterns locked into the economic system come to be challenged and reversed, so as to assert particular assemblages of peasant co-production as outside of the purview of what can be restructured for financial extraction. There are many examples of this approach.

One I have encountered personally is Genuino Clandestino,[26] an Italian network allowing farmers to market products (such as jam or tomato purée) that have been manufactured on the farm, rather than on dedicated processing facilities required by the law. Often, the investment in dedicated processing facilities is not viable for small farmers that cannot rely on enough throughput to justify the expenditure. Hence, although "clandestine"—as they are not produced in legally compliant laboratories—these products are also "genuine," as farmers are accountable to each other and to the broader consumer community (with which they have a direct relationship) for the quality of their products. Genuino Clandestino is itself an illustration of a broader movement of *solidarity-based purchase groups*, which are networks of farmers and consumers, aimed at initiating direct exchanges of agricultural produce for everyday consumption, providing an alternative to supermarket shopping for medium to low income consumers.[27] In this respect, these build on the limitations perceived in other forms of alternative food networks, such as fair trade, and try to improve on the shortcomings encountered in those experiments[28] by going one step further and bypassing big retail to avoid co-optation.

One additional leverage point for systems intervention is paradigm change. As I have shown in Chapter 2, "systems" come to be when the interlocking agencies from which they emerge reach some degree of predictability and recursivity in their inter-actions. This is enabled, in turn, by a certain stability of expecta-tions about agency within the system, and about the relationship of the system to its wider environment. These "stable expectations" define the paradigm after which the system functions, i.e. a certain way of framing the world as an "out there" entity, on which the system acts.

In the current system, a certain view of (unidirectional) causality makes ecological feedback relationships (which are so important in peasant co-production) invisible, and consequently frames food production as a linear input-output process that is open to engineering and packaging into assets.[29] In this paradigm, in which land and biological processes can be broken down and sold, connections are put into place that enable to do just that. As the food system oversteps the limits of sustainability, however, new spaces are opened for paradigms that are more receptive to relationships of mutual causality, where co-production is acknowledged and respected, rather than worked against. In this respect, an interesting effort appears to be that of the permaculture movement. This is a movement that is closely connected to the use of agro-ecological principles in the building of resilient local economies, and which has led to the establishment of the Transition Network, a global web of local communities "in transition" to a model of dwelling that is less taxing on human and ecological resources.[30] In permaculture, the idea is to start with a given vision of the future and a toolbox of ecological principles to facilitate co-production, and subsequently to backcast from that vision and start to create new connections that will lead to the realization of the desired paradigm.[31] Within the Transition Movement, this approach translates into a visioning process that hovers around a paradigm featuring a broader role for agriculture, beyond that of mere "bread basket." A centerpiece of this broader role is ecological stewardship, articulated through—for example—decreased reliance on artificial inputs, as well as improvement in the quality of the soil (so as to enhance its role as a carbon sink to mitigate the problem of climate change).[32] Starting from this vision, a range of initiatives are then put into place that attempt directly to implement it. One of these is the encouragement of self-provision by growing food for home consumption in private or community gardens. Organic urban agriculture can reduce the pressure for productivity on existing local food networks,[33] by making cities self-sufficient to some extent. The case of Cuba's capital Havana meeting most of its fruit and vegetable needs from self-production is often heralded as an example of the weight that urban agriculture can exert.[34] Furthermore, by disentangling food provisioning from transnational networks, localized urban agriculture can also open up new possibilities for farmers in import-dependent developing countries to focus on meeting local demand, rather than produce for export.[35] Another interesting initiative is community-supported agriculture (CSA), which attempts to strengthen direct connections between farmers and the surrounding community. This typically involves provisioning from local farmers, as well as sharing the risk of "bad harvests" (so that payments are made despite fluctuations in the size of the harvest).[36] This type of scheme decreases farmers' dependence on TNC networks (for marketing their produce) or on the financial system (because a stable income requires less reliance on loans). As a consequence, it enables the recovery of peasant metrics of quality,[37] for example by allowing experimentation with organic methods. In fact, since these require a few years to build soil fertility and increase output, they are ill-suited to generate sufficient yields to keep up with loan repayments in the short-term.[38]

"Paradigm shifts" can also be spotted in the enactment of new forms of "conversion," as part of the peasantry's resistance to Empire. What this means, according to Ploeg,[39] is the tracing of connections that are not mediated by money (so that they do not need effectively to be "converted," translated in monetary terms), introducing instead elements of reprocity that manage to mobilize resources that would otherwise go unused, were they to be procured through monetary circuits. A case in point here is the provision of labour for olive harvest, where neighboring peasants help each other in exchange for bottles of olive oil (rather than a monetary wage).[40] These examples—by expressing a symbolic critique of market-mediated relations—effectively challenge the worldview behind the patterning of the current economic system, i.e. that there are "scarce" resources that need to be rationed through markets.[41] Instead, they aim to show that reciprocity and cooperation can, contrary to the assumptions behind the logic of the market, actually enhance the wealth of a community.[42]

Paradigms are therefore another important leverage point, which can be acted upon—through a paradigm shift—to dislodge ingrained expectations and produce new patternings within the system. These paradigm shifts are, of course, complementary to the induction of "learning adaptation" in an existing system through pressure from various external sources. Indeed, learning adaptation requires the presence of internal diversity (such as is sparked by connections guided by an alternative paradigm) in order to enable new responses vis-à-vis old problems.

In sum, even if the food economy may appear as an imposing Leviathan, innovative agency deployed from within and without the system may act as a counterpoint to the existing expansionist tendencies of the financialized economy. Equally important is the fact that it is only in a worldview that is systematically oblivious to ecological feedback relationships—perhaps shunning them as an inhospitable state of nature of the sort imagined by Hobbes[43]—that monsters such as the Leviathan find their home. A new story of food as co-production can, therefore, make a difference. This story should actually have many different versions, depending on the particular set of micro-conditions in which food production takes place. The struggle for food sovereignty, understood precisely as the development of as many different stories of food as there are local natural and human ecologies,[44] is therefore an important part of the work ahead.

Endnotes

Chapter 1

1 Thomas Hobbes, *Leviathan or the Matter, Forme & Power of a Commonwealth Ecclesiasticall and Civil* (London: Andrew Cooke, 1651), http://bit.ly/hobbes_leviath (accessed July 23, 2012).

2 Raj Patel, *The Value of Nothing: How to Reshape Market Society and Redefine Democracy* (London: Portobello Books, 2010), 87–89.

3 I use "agency" here in the very broad sense of "making someone do something," i.e. triggering a response in other actors (Bruno Latour, *Reassembling the Social: An Introduction to Actor-Network Theory* (Oxford: Oxford University Press, 2005), 107).

4 Michael Hardt and Antonio Negri, *Empire* (Cambridge, MA: Harvard University Press, 2001).

5 Jan Douwe van der Ploeg, *The New Peasantries: Struggles for Autonomy and Sustainability in an Era of Empire and Globalization* (London: Earthscan, 2009), 236.

6 Joanna Macy, *Mutual Causality in Buddhism and General Systems Theory* (Albany: State University of New York Press, 1991).

7 Latour, *Reassembling the Social: An Introduction to Actor-Network Theory*, 57.

Chapter 2

1 Ben Anderson and Paul Harrison, "The Promise of Non-Representational Theories," in *Taking-Place: Non-Representational Theories and Geography*, ed. Ben Anderson and Paul Harrison (Farnham: Ashgate, 2010), 18.

2 Donella H. Meadows, *Thinking in Systems: A Primer*, ed. Diana Wright (London: Earthscan, 2009), 4.

3 Macy, *Mutual Causality in Buddhism and General Systems*

Theory, 72.

4 Hans-Georg Moeller, *Luhmann Explained: From Souls to Systems* (Peru, IL: Open Court, 2006), 21.

5 Gunther Teubner, "The Anonymous Matrix: Human Rights Violations by 'Private' Transnational Actors," *Modern Law Review* 69, no. 3 (2006): 333.

6 Alex Viskovatoff, "Foundations of Niklas Luhmann's Theory of Social Systems," *Philosophy of the Social Sciences* 29, no. 4 (1999): 498 & 503.

7 For the sake of rigour, I am aware that this is not—from a Luhmannian perspective—a "purist" definition of system, in that it opens a space for agency. In so doing, however, it is consistent with the intuition that I develop in this book, namely that, while systems can be thought of as an anonymous matrix on which individual actors have no control, they are simultaneously affected by the interlocking sets of agencies enmeshed in this matrix.

8 David Seidl, *Luhmann's Theory of Autopoietic Social Systems*, Working Paper (Munich: Munich School of Management, 2004), 8–9, http://bit.ly/seidl2004 (accessed January 8, 2012).

9 Moeller, *Luhmann Explained*, 22–23; see also Helmut Willke, "The Autonomy of the Financial System: Symbolic Coupling and the Language of Capital," in *Towards a Cognitive Mode in Global Finance: The Governance of a Knowledge-based Financial System*, ed. Torsten Strulik and Helmut Willke (Frankfurt/New York: Campus Verlag, 2006), 58.

10 Viskovatoff, "Foundations of Niklas Luhmann's Theory of Social Systems," 500–501.

11 Moeller, *Luhmann Explained*, 23–24.

12 Niklas Luhmann, *Ecological Communication*, trans. John Jr. Bednarz (Chicago: University of Chicago Press, 1989), 36 & 52.

13 Jens Beckert, *Beyond the Market: The Social Foundations of Economic Efficiency*, trans. Barbara Harshav (Princeton:

Princeton University Press, 2002), 215.

14   Elena Esposito, *The Future of Futures: The Time of Money in Financing and Society* (Cheltenham: Edward Elgar, 2011), 124.

15   Willke, "The Autonomy of the Financial System: Symbolic Coupling and the Language of Capital," 46.

16   Meadows, *Thinking in Systems: A Primer*, 14.

17   Moeller, *Luhmann Explained*, 24.

18   Ibid., 22.

19   Niklas Luhmann, "Operational Closure and Structural Coupling: the Differentiation of the Legal System," *Cardozo Law Review* 13 (1991-92): 1420.

20   Moeller, *Luhmann Explained*, 36.

21   Ibid., 14.

22   Interestingly, the presence of different kinds of systems that "leave out" different sorts of extra-systemic relations means that each of them demarcates a different environment, so that the idea that there exists a common reality observable from different systems has to be discarded: each system creates its own environment by virtue of its closure (Ibid., 16).

23   Ibid., 14.

24   Macy, *Mutual Causality in Buddhism and General Systems Theory*, 92.

25   Moeller, *Luhmann Explained*, 37.

26   Macy, *Mutual Causality in Buddhism and General Systems Theory*, 76.

27   Ibid., 96.

28   Meadows, *Thinking in Systems: A Primer*, 30–31.

29   Macy, *Mutual Causality in Buddhism and General Systems Theory*, 73; Willke, "The Autonomy of the Financial System: Symbolic Coupling and the Language of Capital," 44.

30   Robert Biel, *The Entropy of Capitalism* (Leiden: Brill, 2011), 166.

31   Alexandra Hessling and Hanno Pahl, "The Global System of

Finance: Scanning Talcott Parsons and Niklas Luhmann for Theoretical Keystones," *American Journal of Economics and Sociology* 65, no. 1 (2006): 207.

32 Beckert, *Beyond the Market*, 212.

33 Hessling and Pahl, "The Global System of Finance: Scanning Talcott Parsons and Niklas Luhmann for Theoretical Keystones," 191.

34 Luciano Gallino, *Finanzcapitalismo: La Civiltà del Denaro in Crisi* (Turin: Einaudi, 2011), 7.

35 Duncan Wigan, "Financialisation and Derivatives: The Political Construction of an Artifice of Indifference," *Competition and Change* 13, no. 2 (2009): 162.

36 Esposito, *The Future of Futures*, 125.

37 Willke, "The Autonomy of the Financial System: Symbolic Coupling and the Language of Capital," 53.

38 Moeller, *Luhmann Explained*, 26.

39 Beckert, *Beyond the Market*, 214; Ricardo de Medeiros Carneiro et al., "The Fourth Dimension: Derivatives in a Capitalism With Financial Dominance" (presented at the "Political Economy and the Outlook for Capitalism" Conference, Paris: Association Française d'Économie Politique, 2012), 8, http://bit.ly/fourth_dimension (accessed August 13, 2012).

40 Willke, "The Autonomy of the Financial System: Symbolic Coupling and the Language of Capital," 51.

41 Hessling and Pahl, "The Global System of Finance: Scanning Talcott Parsons and Niklas Luhmann for Theoretical Keystones," 207–208.

42 Brian Rotman, *Signifying Nothing: The Semiotics of Zero* (Stanford: Stanford University Press, 1993), 5, quoted in Dick Bryan and Michael Rafferty, "Financial Derivatives and the Theory of Money," *Economy and Society* 36, no. 1 (2007): 138.

43 Dick Bryan and Michael Rafferty, *Capitalism with Derivatives:*

A Political Economy of Financial Derivatives, Capital and Class (Basingstoke: Palgrave Macmillan, 2006), 11.

44 Bryan and Rafferty, "Financial Derivatives and the Theory of Money," 149; Bryan and Rafferty, *Capitalism with Derivatives: A Political Economy of Financial Derivatives, Capital and Class,* 154; see also Esposito, *The Future of Futures,* 126.

45 Bryan and Rafferty, "Financial Derivatives and the Theory of Money," 141.

46 Ibid.

47 Ibid., 142.

48 Wigan, "Financialisation and Derivatives: The Political Construction of an Artifice of Indifference," 167.

49 Edward LiPuma and Benjamin Lee, "Financial Derivatives and the Rise of Circulation," *Economy and Society* 34, no. 3 (2005): 414 & 423; Edward LiPuma and Benjamin Lee, *Financial Derivatives and the Globalization of Risk* (Durham & London: Duke University Press, 2004), 148 & 150.

50 Dick Bryan and Michael Rafferty, "Financial Derivatives: Bubble or Anchor?," in *Global Finance in the New Century,* ed. Libby Assassi, Anastasia Nesvetailova, and Duncan Wigan (Basingstoke: Palgrave Macmillan, 2007), 34; Bryan and Rafferty, *Capitalism with Derivatives: A Political Economy of Financial Derivatives, Capital and Class,* 35.

51 Bryan and Rafferty, "Financial Derivatives: Bubble or Anchor?," 34.

52 Christian Marazzi, *The Violence of Financial Capitalism,* trans. Kristina Lebedeva and Jason Francis McGimsey (Boston: Semiotext(e), 2011), 30.

53 Meadows, *Thinking in Systems: A Primer,* 135.

54 Gunther Teubner, "A Constitutional Moment? The Logics of 'Hitting the Bottom'," in *The Financial Crisis in Constitutional Perspective,* ed. Poul Kjaer, Gunther Teubner, and Alberto Febbrajo (Oxford: Hart Publishing, 2011).

55 Biel, *The Entropy of Capitalism*; Robert Biel, "The Political

Economy of Food – Towards an Entropy-Based Systems Analysis of the Current Crisis and Its Solution" (presented at the "Political Economy and the Outlook for Capitalism" Conference, Paris: Association Française d'Économie Politique, 2012), http://bit.ly/biel2012 (accessed July 30, 2012).

56 Macy, *Mutual Causality in Buddhism and General Systems Theory*, 126.

57 Biel, "The Political Economy of Food – Towards an Entropy-Based Systems Analysis of the Current Crisis and Its Solution," 2 & 14.

58 Teubner, "A Constitutional Moment? The Logics of 'Hitting the Bottom'," 8.

59 Esposito, *The Future of Futures*, 125.

60 Willke, "The Autonomy of the Financial System: Symbolic Coupling and the Language of Capital," 54–55; Hanno Pahl, "On the Unity and Difference of Finance and the Economy: Investigations for a New Sociology of Money," in *Towards a Cognitive Mode in Global Finance: The Governance of a Knowledge-based Financial System*, ed. Torsten Strulik and Helmut Willke (Frankfurt/New York: Campus, 2006), 96–97.

61 Biel, *The Entropy of Capitalism*, 266.

62 Robert Boyer, "Capitalism Strikes Back: Why and What Consequences for Social Sciences?," *Revue de la régulation* 1 (2007): 34 ff., http://bit.ly/boyer_2007 (accessed July 25, 2012).

63 Biel, *The Entropy of Capitalism*, 298.

64 Peter Rossman and Gerard Greenfield, "Financialization: New Routes to Profit, New Challenges for Trade Unions," *Labour Education* 142, no. 1 (2006): 5, http://bit.ly/rossman_greenfield (accessed July 23, 2012).

65 Ugo Mattei and Laura Nader, *Plunder: When the Rule of Law is Illegal* (Oxford: Wiley-Blackwell, 2008), 4.

66 Biel, *The Entropy of Capitalism*, 157–159, 162–163 & 208.

67 Geoffrey Ingham, *Capitalism* (Cambridge: Polity, 2008), 173.

68 Anastasia Nesvetailova, *Financial Alchemy in Crisis: The Great Liquidity Illusion* (London: Pluto Press, 2010), 13.

69 Anastasia Nesvetailova, *Fragile Finance: Debt, Speculation and Crisis in the Age of Global Credit* (Basingstoke: Palgrave Macmillan, 2007), 78.

70 Latour, *Reassembling the Social: An Introduction to Actor-Network Theory*, 102–103; see also Viskovatoff, "Foundations of Niklas Luhmann's Theory of Social Systems," 496.

71 Donald MacKenzie, *Material Markets: How Economic Agents are Constructed* (Oxford: Oxford University Press, 2008), 13–16.

72 Latour, *Reassembling the Social: An Introduction to Actor-Network Theory*, 68–70.

73 Hessling and Pahl, "The Global System of Finance: Scanning Talcott Parsons and Niklas Luhmann for Theoretical Keystones," 209 ff.

74 Hessling and Pahl, "The Global System of Finance: Scanning Talcott Parsons and Niklas Luhmann for Theoretical Keystones."

75 Karin Knorr Cetina and Urs Bruegger, "Global Microstructures: The Virtual Societies of Financial Markets," *American Journal of Sociology* 107, no. 4 (2002): 905–950.

76 Andrew Leyshon and Nigel Thrift, *Money/Space: Geographies of Monetary Transformation* (London: Routledge, 1997), 348.

77 MacKenzie, *Material Markets*, 12.

78 Knorr Cetina and Bruegger, "Global Microstructures: The Virtual Societies of Financial Markets," 923.

79 Ibid., 924.

80 Leyshon and Thrift, *Money/Space*, 344.

81 Hessling and Pahl, "The Global System of Finance: Scanning Talcott Parsons and Niklas Luhmann for Theoretical Keystones," 210.

82 MacKenzie, *Material Markets*, 66.

83 Peter Robbins, "Tropical Commodities as Tradeable Assets: An Interview with Peter Robbins," interview by Luigi Russi, March 26, 2012, http://bit.ly/robbins_interv (accessed July 23, 2012).

84 MacKenzie, *Material Markets*, 92.

85 Ibid., 78–83.

86 Leyshon and Thrift, *Money/Space*, 345.

87 Knorr Cetina and Bruegger, "Global Microstructures: The Virtual Societies of Financial Markets," 915.

88 Hessling and Pahl, "The Global System of Finance: Scanning Talcott Parsons and Niklas Luhmann for Theoretical Keystones," 210.

89 Eugene Fama, "Efficient Capital Markets: A Review of Theory and Empirical Work," *Journal of Finance* 25 (1970): 383–417.

90 Hessling and Pahl, "The Global System of Finance: Scanning Talcott Parsons and Niklas Luhmann for Theoretical Keystones," 210.

91 Robert Sollis, *Empirical Finance for Finance and Banking* (Chichester: Wiley, 2012), 18 ff.

92 Emmanuel Didier, "Do Statistics 'Perform' the Economy?," in *Do Economists Make Markets? On the Performativity of Economics*, ed. Donald MacKenzie, Fabian Muniesa, and Lucia Siu (Princeton: Princeton University Press, 2007), 307–308.

93 Joel Kurtzman, *The Death of Money* (New York: Simon & Schuster, 1993), 145.

94 Donald MacKenzie, "Is Economics Performative? Option Theory and the Construction of Derivatives Markets," in *Do Economists Make Markets? On the Performativity of Economics*, ed. Donald MacKenzie, Fabian Muniesa, and Lucia Siu (Princeton: Princeton University Press, 2007), 54–86.

95 Gallino, *Finanzcapitalismo: La Civiltà del Denaro in Crisi*, 138.

96 Kurtzman, *The Death of Money*, 161.

97 Hessling and Pahl, "The Global System of Finance: Scanning Talcott Parsons and Niklas Luhmann for Theoretical Keystones," 211–212.

98 Ibid., 214.

99 Andreas Fischer-Lescano and Gunther Teubner, "Regime-Collisions: The Vain Search for Legal Unity in the Fragmentation of Global Law," trans. Michelle Everson, *Michigan Journal of International Law* 4 (2004): 1018.

100 Hessling and Pahl, "The Global System of Finance: Scanning Talcott Parsons and Niklas Luhmann for Theoretical Keystones," 212.

101 Nigel Thrift, *Knowing Capitalism* (London: SAGE, 2005), 175.

102 Ibid., quoting Michael D. Schrage, *Serious Play: How the World's Best Companies Simulate to Innovate* (Cambridge, MA: Harvard Business School Press, 2000), 46–47.

103 Thrift, *Knowing Capitalism*, 134.

104 Angelo Salento and Giovanni Masino, "Financialization and Organizational Change: A Comparative Study on Multinational Enterprises," in *CMS7 2011 7th International Critical Management Studies Conference Proceedings* (presented at the 7th International Critical Management Studies Conference, Naples: Faculty of Economics, University of Naples Federico II, 2011), http://bit.ly/salento_masino (accessed July 23, 2012).

105 Ibid., 4.

106 Thrift, *Knowing Capitalism*, 147.

107 Ibid., 149.

108 Ibid.

109 Anderson and Harrison, "The Promise of Non-Representational Theories," 7.

110 Karen Ho, "Disciplining Investment Bankers, Disciplining the Economy: Wall Street's Institutional Culture of Crisis and the Downsizing of American Corporations," *American Anthropologist* 111, no. 2 (2009): 179 & 184–185.

111 Ibid., 179.

112 Ibid., 186.

113 Ibid., 180.

114 Ibid., 186.

115 Gerald A. Epstein, "Introduction: Financialization and the World Economy," in *Financialization and the World Economy*, ed. Gerald A. Epstein (Cheltenham: Edward Elgar, 2006), 3.

116 Salento and Masino, "Financialization and Organizational Change: A Comparative Study on Multinational Enterprises," 4.

117 Ibid., 6.

118 Hessling and Pahl, "The Global System of Finance: Scanning Talcott Parsons and Niklas Luhmann for Theoretical Keystones," 214.

119 Greta R. Krippner, "The Financialization of the American Economy," *Socio-Economic Review* 3 (2005): 201.

120 Biel, *The Entropy of Capitalism*, 304.

121 George Soros, *The New Paradigm for Financial Markets: The Credit Crisis of 2008 and What It Means* (New York: PublicAffairs, 2008), 29 ff.

122 George Soros, *The Alchemy of Finance: Reading the Mind of the Market* (New York: John Wiley & Sons, 1994), 423–424.

123 Anderson and Harrison, "The Promise of Non-Representational Theories," 20.

124 Harriet Friedmann, "Distance and Durability: Shaky Foundations of the World Food Economy," in *The Global Restructuring of Agro-Food Systems*, ed. Philip McMichael (Ithaca: Cornell University Press, 1994), 273.

Chapter 3

1 Jennifer Clapp, *Food* (Cambridge: Polity, 2012), 44 ff.

2 John Bellamy Foster, *The Vulnerable Planet: A Short Economic History of the Environment* (New York: Monthly Review Press, 1999), 121–122.

3   See Willke, "The Autonomy of the Financial System: Symbolic Coupling and the Language of Capital," 47.

4   Miguel Altieri, *Agroecology: The Science of Sustainable Agriculture*, 2nd ed. (London: Intermediate Technology Publications, 1995), 1.

5   Ploeg, *The New Peasantries*, 23–26.

6   Anthony Weis, "The Accelerating Biophysical Contradictions of Industrial Capitalist Agriculture.," *Journal of Agrarian Change* 10, no. 3 (July 2010): 335.

7   Vandana Shiva, *Stolen Harvest: The Hijacking of the Global Food Supply* (Cambridge, MA: South End Press, 1999), 7–8; La Via Campesina, *Sustainable Peasant and Family Farm Agriculture Can Feed the World* (Jakarta: La Via Campesina, September 2010), 4–5, http://bit.ly/viacampesina_2010 (accessed July 23, 2012).

8   Foster, *The Vulnerable Planet*, 124.

9   Clapp, *Food*, 11.

10 Ploeg, *The New Peasantries*, 25–26; Walden Bello, *The Food Wars* (London: Verso, 2009), 25–26; Philip McMichael, "Global Development and the Corporate Food Regime," in *New Directions in the Sociology of Global Development*, ed. Frederick H. Buttel and Philip McMichael, vol. 11, Research in Rural Sociology and Development (Amsterdam: Elsevier, 2005), 287, http://bit.ly/mcmichael_2005 (accessed July 23, 2012).

11 Bello, *The Food Wars*, 22.

12 Ibid.

13 Peter Atkins and Ian Bowler, *Food in Society: Economy, Culture, Geography* (London: Arnold, 2001), 25.

14 Harriet Friedmann and Philip McMichael, "Agriculture and the State System," *Sociologia Ruralis* 29, no. 2 (1989): 81–82.

15 Ibid., 80–81.

16 Clapp, *Food*, 33.

17 David Goodman, Bernardo Sorj, and John Wilkinson, *From*

Farming to Biotechnology: A Theory of Agro-Industrial Development (Oxford: Blackwell, 1987), 8.

18 Ibid., 58.

19 Ibid., 69.

20 Clapp, *Food*, 30–31.

21 Ibid., 34.

22 Atkins and Bowler, *Food in Society*, 28.

23 Philip McMichael, *Development and Social Change*, 4th ed. (Los Angeles: Pine Forge Press, 2008), 81.

24 Tim Lang, David Barling, and Martin Caraher, *Food Policy: Integrating Health, Environment and Society* (Oxford: Oxford University Press, 2009), 27 ff.

25 Tim Lang and Michael Heasman, *Food Wars: the Global Battle for Mouths, Minds and Markets* (London: Earthscan, 2004), 19–20.

26 Clapp, *Food*, 46–47.

27 Raj Patel, *Stuffed and Starved* (London: Portobello Books, 2007), 93.

28 Yanis Varoufakis, Joseph Halevi, and Nicholas Theocarakis, *Modern Political Economics: Making Sense of the Post-2008 World* (London: Routledge, 2011), 304–306.

29 Thomas Lines, *Making Poverty: A History* (London: Zed Books, 2008), 38–43.

30 A digression should be made here about the process of decolonization that took place after World War II. At this time, in fact, the former colonized lands were endowed with the sovereignty that put them on par with the former colonial masters. However, as outlined by a growing group of critical legal scholars, the bestowment of sovereignty upon former colonies only translated in opening up new possibilities of exploitation cloaked in the language of formally egalitarian relations between sovereigns (Antony Anghie, *Imperialism, Sovereignty and the Making of International Law* (Cambridge: Cambridge University Press,

2004); China Miéville, "The Commodity-Form Theory of International Law," in *International Law on the Left: Re-Examining Marxist Legacies*, ed. Susan Marks (Cambridge: Cambridge University Press, 2008), 92–132). In the case of SAPs, in fact, forced liberalization under the stick of conditionality has been regarded as yet another form of the colonial enterprise dubbed "neo-colonialism" (Mattei and Nader, *Plunder*, 28 ff.).

31 Michael J. Trebilcock and Robert Howse, *The Regulation of International Trade*, 2nd ed. (London: Routledge, 1999), 20–21 & 35.

32 Clapp, *Food*, 73.

33 Ibid., 74.

34 Shiva, *Stolen Harvest*, 7.

35 David Burch and Geoffrey Lawrence, "Towards a Third Food Regime: Behind the Transformation," *Agriculture and Human Values* 26 (2009): 275–277.

36 Clapp, *Food*, 90 ff.

37 Luis Llambi, "Opening Economies and Closing Markets: Latin American Agriculture's Difficult Search for a Place in the Emerging Global Order," in *From Columbus to ConAgra: The Globalization of Agriculture and Food*, ed. Alessandro Bonanno et al. (Lawrence: University Press of Kansas, 1994), 190.

38 Philip McMichael and Harriet Friedmann, "Situating the 'Retailing Revolution'," in *Supermarkets and Agri-Food Supply Chains*, ed. David Burch and Geoffrey Lawrence (Cheltenham: Edward Elgar, 2007), 302–304.

39 Ploeg, *The New Peasantries*, 256.

40 Bryan and Rafferty, "Financial Derivatives: Bubble or Anchor?".

41 Ploeg, *The New Peasantries*, 257.

42 Clapp, *Food*.

43 Burch and Lawrence, "Towards a Third Food Regime:

Behind the Transformation," 275.

44 Weis, "The Accelerating Biophysical Contradictions of Industrial Capitalist Agriculture.," 334 ff.; Ploeg, *The New Peasantries*, 271–273; Bello, *The Food Wars*, 137–139.

45 Anthony Weis, *The Global Food Economy: The Battle for the Future of Farming* (London: Zed Books, 2007), 165.

46 Bello, *The Food Wars*, 134.

47 Alessandro Bonanno and Douglas H. Constance, *Stories of Globalization: Transnational Corporations, Resistance, and the State* (University Park, PA: Pennsylvania State University Press, 2008), 9.

48 Clapp, *Food*, 161.

Chapter 4

1 Jayati Ghosh, *Commodity Speculation and the Food Crisis*, Briefing (World Development Movement, October 2010), http://bit.ly/ghosh_wdm (accessed July 23, 2012).

2 Thijs Kerckhoffs, Roos van Os, and Myriam Vander Stichele, *Financing Food: Financialisation and Financial Actors in Agriculture Commodity Markets*, SOMO Paper (Amsterdam: Centre for Research on Multinational Corporations, April 2010), 7, http://bit.ly/kerckhoffs (accessed July 23, 1923).

3 Eric Holt-Gimenez and Raj Patel, *Food Rebellions: Crisis and the Hunger for Justice* (Oxford: Pambazuka Press, 2009), 6.

4 Jean Ziegler, *Destruction Massive: Géopolitique de la Faim* (Paris: Seuil, 2011), 299 ff.

5 C.P. Chandrasekhar and Jayati Ghosh, "Another Looming Food Crisis," *The Hindu Business Line*, July 23, 2012, http://bit.ly/ghosh_chandr (accessed August 3, 2012).

6 Clapp, *Food*, 130; Jayati Ghosh, "The Unnatural Coupling: Food and Global Finance," *Journal of Agrarian Change* 10, no. 1 (2010): 72–73.

7 Olivier De Schutter, *Food Commodities Speculation and Food Price Crises*, Briefing Note (UN Special Rapporteur on the

Right to Food, September 2010), 3.

8   Kerckhoffs, van Os, and Vander Stichele, *Financing Food: Financialisation and Financial Actors in Agriculture Commodity Markets*, 2.

9   Peter Robbins, *Stolen Fruit: The Tropical Commodities Disaster* (London: Zed Books, 2003), 167–168.

10 Anne E. Peck, "The Economic Role of Traditional Commodity Futures Markets," in *Futures Markets: Their Economic Role*, ed. Anne E. Peck (Washington D.C.: American Enterprise Institute for Public Policy Research, 1985), 4–7.

11 Frederick Kaufman, "The Food Bubble: How Wall Street Starved Millions and Got Away With It," *Harper's Magazine*, July 2010, 30.

12 De Schutter, *Food Commodities Speculation and Food Price Crises*, 9.

13 Kaufman, "The Food Bubble: How Wall Street Starved Millions and Got Away With It," 30.

14 Carley Garner, *A Trader's First Book on Commodities* (Upper Saddle River, NJ: FT Press, 2010), 25.

15 Ibid., 26.

16 Ibid., 25.

17 Michael W. Masters and Adam K. White, *How Institutional Investors Are Driving Up Food And Energy Prices*, Special Report (The Accidental Hunt Brothers, July 31, 2008), 2, http://bit.ly/masters_white (accessed July 23, 2012).

18 Kaufman, "The Food Bubble: How Wall Street Starved Millions and Got Away With It," 30.

19 Alan Bjerga, "How Goldman Sachs Started the Food Speculation Frenzy," *The Ecologist*, September 13, 2011, http://bit.ly/bjerga_gs (accessed July 23, 2012); Kaufman, "The Food Bubble: How Wall Street Starved Millions and Got Away With It," 31.

20 Kerckhoffs, van Os, and Vander Stichele, *Financing Food: Financialisation and Financial Actors in Agriculture Commodity*

Markets, 5.

21 Masters and White, *How Institutional Investors Are Driving Up Food And Energy Prices*, 8.

22 David Frenk and Wallace Turbeville, *Commodity Index Traders and the Boom/Bust Cycle in Commodities Prices*, Anthropic Finance and Better Markets: Toward a New Understanding of How Markets Function and the Role They Serve in Society (Washington D.C.: Better Markets, 2011), 8, http://bit.ly/fr_turbeville (accessed July 23, 2012).

23 Ibid., 9.

24 De Schutter, *Food Commodities Speculation and Food Price Crises*, 9.

25 Masters and White, *How Institutional Investors Are Driving Up Food And Energy Prices*, 9.

26 Frenk and Turbeville, *Commodity Index Traders and the Boom/Bust Cycle in Commodities Prices*, 8.

27 Garner, *A Trader's First Book on Commodities*, 28.

28 David Frenk and Michael W. Masters, *Anthropic Finance: How Markets Function*, Anthropic Finance and Better Markets: Toward a New Understanding of How Markets Function and the Role They Serve in Society (Washington D.C.: Better Markets, 2010), 50, http://bit.ly/frenk_masters (accessed July 23, 2012).

29 Masters and White, *How Institutional Investors Are Driving Up Food And Energy Prices*, 34.

30 Kerckhoffs, van Os, and Vander Stichele, *Financing Food: Financialisation and Financial Actors in Agriculture Commodity Markets*, 4.

31 Ghosh, "The Unnatural Coupling: Food and Global Finance," 78.

32 De Schutter, *Food Commodities Speculation and Food Price Crises*, 5.

33 Frenk and Turbeville, *Commodity Index Traders and the Boom/Bust Cycle in Commodities Prices*, 9.

34 Thomas Lines, *Speculation in Food Commodity Markets* (World Development Movement, April 2010), 14–15, http://bit.ly/lines_commodity (accessed July 23, 2012).

35 United Nations Commission on Trade and Development Secretariat, *Price Formation in Financialized Commodity Markets: The Role of Information* (New York-Geneva: United Nations, June 2011), 19.

36 Cornelia Staritz, *Financial Markets and the Commodity Price Boom: Causes and Implications for Developing Countries* (Vienna: Oesterreichische Forschungsstiftung fuer Internationale Entwicklung, April 2012), 13, http://bit.ly /staritz (accessed July 23, 2012); John M. Talbot, "Information, Finance and the New International Inequality: The Case of Coffee," *Journal of World-Systems Research* 8, no. 2 (2002): 231–232.

37 A. Jason Windawi, *Speculation, Embedding and Food Prices: A Cointegration Analysis*, Working Paper, Institute for Social and Economic Research and Policy (New York: Columbia University, February 2012), 16 & 20, http://bit.ly/windawi (accessed July 23, 2012).

38 Frenk and Turbeville, *Commodity Index Traders and the Boom/Bust Cycle in Commodities Prices*, 30.

39 Kaufman, "The Food Bubble: How Wall Street Starved Millions and Got Away With It," 30.

40 Frenk and Turbeville, *Commodity Index Traders and the Boom/Bust Cycle in Commodities Prices*, 6.

41 De Schutter, *Food Commodities Speculation and Food Price Crises*, 4.

42 Frenk and Turbeville, *Commodity Index Traders and the Boom/Bust Cycle in Commodities Prices*.

43 Ibid., 10.

44 Javier Blas, "Commodity Indices: 'Rollover' Practice Hits Investors," *Financial Times*, November 1, 2009, http://bit.ly/blas_roll (accessed July 23, 2012).

45 Staritz, *Financial Markets and the Commodity Price Boom: Causes and Implications for Developing Countries*, 11; Ghosh, "The Unnatural Coupling: Food and Global Finance," 28.

46 Robert J. Greer, "The Nature of Commodity Index Returns," *The Journal of Alternative Investments* 3, no. 1 (2000): 46; Masters and White, *How Institutional Investors Are Driving Up Food And Energy Prices*, 9.

47 Yiqun Mou, "Limits to Arbitrage and Commodity Index Investment" (PhD Dissertation, New York: Columbia University, 2011), 6, http://bit.ly/mou_2011 (accessed July 23, 2012).

48 Frenk and Turbeville, *Commodity Index Traders and the Boom/Bust Cycle in Commodities Prices*, 13.

49 J. Bradford De Long et al., "Positive Feedback Investment Staregies and Destabilizing Rational Speculation," *The Journal of Finance* 45, no. 2 (June 1990): 394.

50 Frenk and Turbeville, *Commodity Index Traders and the Boom/Bust Cycle in Commodities Prices*, 17; De Schutter, *Food Commodities Speculation and Food Price Crises*, 4.

51 Scott H. Irwin, Dwight R. Sanders, and Robert P. Merrin, "Devil or Angel? The Role of Speculation in the Recent Commodity Price Boom (and Bust)," *Journal of Agricultural and Applied Economics* 41, no. 2 (August 2009): 379–380.

52 Frenk and Turbeville, *Commodity Index Traders and the Boom/Bust Cycle in Commodities Prices*, 9.

53 Ibid., 11.

54 Ibid., 29; Frenk and Masters, *Anthropic Finance: How Markets Function*, 30.

55 Frenk and Turbeville, *Commodity Index Traders and the Boom/Bust Cycle in Commodities Prices*, 29; Frenk and Masters, *Anthropic Finance: How Markets Function*, 44.

56 Ghosh, "The Unnatural Coupling: Food and Global Finance," 79.

57 Ibid., 81.

Chapter 5

1   Ploeg, *The New Peasantries*, 24.

2   Ibid., 23.

3   Ibid., 269.

4   Ibid., 117–118.

5   Ibid., 24.

6   Colin Tudge, *Feeding People is Easy* (Pari: Pari Publishing, 2007), 39–40; Michael Carolan, *The Sociology of Food and Agriculture* (London: Earthscan, 2012), 205.

7   Biel, "The Political Economy of Food – Towards an Entropy-Based Systems Analysis of the Current Crisis and Its Solution," 5.

8   Carolan, *The Sociology of Food and Agriculture*, 206–207.

9   Tudge, *Feeding People is Easy*, 58.

10 Henry Bernstein, " 'The Peasantry' in Global Capitalism: Who, Where and Why?," *Socialist Register* 37 (2001): 27.

11 Ibid., 28.

12 David Goodman and Michael Redclift, *Refashioning Nature: Food, Ecology and Culture* (London: Routledge, 1991), 71.

13 Ibid., 96.

14 Bernstein, " 'The Peasantry' in Global Capitalism: Who, Where and Why?," 35–36.

15 Ploeg, *The New Peasantries*, 39 & 42, quoting John Harriss, *Rural Development: Theories of Peasant Economy and Agrarian Change* (London: Hutchinson, 1982), 22; see also Giuliano Girelli, *The Last Farmer*, Documentary (M.A.I.S. ong, 2012), http://vimeo.com/38351098 (accessed July 23, 2012).

16 Bernstein, " 'The Peasantry' in Global Capitalism: Who, Where and Why?," 28.

17 Ploeg, *The New Peasantries*, 114.

18 Lang and Heasman, *Food Wars: the Global Battle for Mouths, Minds and Markets*, 148.

19 Ploeg, *The New Peasantries*, 129.

20 Neil Ward, "The Agricultural Treadmill and the Rural

Environment in the Post-Productivist Era," *Sociologia Ruralis* 33, no. 3–4 (1993): 358; Lines, *Making Poverty*, 73.

21 Ploeg, *The New Peasantries*, 127.

22 Sigmund Borgan, "Agricultural Policy in Western Europe and Some of Its Sociological Aspects," *Sociologia Ruralis* 9, no. 3 (1969): 252–260.

23 Michael Rowbotham, *The Grip of Death: A Study of Modern Money, Debt Slavery and Destructive Economics* (Charlbury: Jon Carpenter, 1998), 119.

24 Weis, "The Accelerating Biophysical Contradictions of Industrial Capitalist Agriculture.," 316; Tudge, *Feeding People is Easy*, 102–104.

25 Tudge, *Feeding People is Easy*, 123.

26 Rowbotham, *The Grip of Death: A Study of Modern Money, Debt Slavery and Destructive Economics*, 114.

27 Rebecca Laughton, *Surviving and Thriving on the Land* (Totnes: Green Books, 2008), 51.

28 Ploeg, *The New Peasantries*, 131–132.

29 Ibid., 49.

30 Ibid., 126 & 129.

31 Ibid., 134.

32 Ibid., 72–73.

33 Ibid., 220.

34 I am grateful to Roberto Schellino for pointing this out to me.

35 Bernd van der Meulen, *Reconciling Food Law to Competitiveness: Report of the Regulatory Environment of the European Food and Dairy Sector* (Wageningen: Wageningen Academic Publishers, 2009), 66.

36 Ibid., 67.

37 Nicola Angrisano, *Genuino Clandestino: Movimento di Resistenze Contadine*, Documentary (InsuTv, 2011), http://vimeo.com/34322825 (accessed July 23, 2012).

38 Meulen, *Reconciling Food Law to Competitiveness*, 67.

39 Artisan Forum, *The New Hygiene Regulations and Speciality Food Production* (Dublin: Food Safety Authority of Ireland, August 2005), 15, http://bit.ly/Artisan_Forum (accessed July 26, 2012).

40 Tudge, *Feeding People is Easy*, 101–104.

41 Biel, *The Entropy of Capitalism*, 304; Marazzi, *The Violence of Financial Capitalism*, 117.

42 Bonanno and Constance, *Stories of Globalization: Transnational Corporations, Resistance, and the State*, 37.

43 Amit Thorat, *Rising Market Control of Transnational Agribusiness*, Focus (New Delhi: International Development Economics Associates, 2003), 1, http://bit.ly/thorat_TNCs (accessed July 23, 2012).

44 Ibid., 9.

45 Lang and Heasman, *Food Wars: the Global Battle for Mouths, Minds and Markets*, 144.

46 Ploeg, *The New Peasantries*, 87 ff.

47 Ibid., 243.

48 Ibid., 246.

49 Ibid.; see also Marazzi, *The Violence of Financial Capitalism*, 41.

50 Aravind Ganesh, "The Right to Food and Buyer Power," *German Law Journal* 11, no. 11 (2010): 1195–1196; Ploeg, *The New Peasantries*, 239.

51 Brewster Kneen, "Restructuring Food for Corporate Profit: The Corporate Genetics of Cargill and Monsanto," *Agriculture and Human Values* 16, no. 2 (1999): 161.

52 Tiziana Terranova, "New Economy, Financialization and Social Production in the Web 2.0," in *Crisis in the Global Economy: Financial Markets, Social Struggles and New Political Scenarios*, ed. Andrea Fumagalli and Sandro Mezzadra, trans. Jason Francis McGimsey (Los Angeles: Semiotext(e), 2010), 155.

53 IUF, *Feeding Financial Markets: Financialization and Restructuring in Nestlé, Kraft and Unilever* (International

Union of Food, Agricultural, Hotel, Restaurant, Catering, Tobacco and Allied Workers' Associations, October 2006), 9–10, http://bit.ly/IUF_finance (accessed July 23, 2012).

54 Marazzi, *The Violence of Financial Capitalism*, 54.

55 IUF, *Feeding Financial Markets: Financialization and Restructuring in Nestlé, Kraft and Unilever*, 10.

56 Burch and Lawrence, "Towards a Third Food Regime: Behind the Transformation," 277.

57 Peter Rossman, "What Financialization Means for Food Workers," *Seedling*, 2010, 25.

58 Rowbotham, *The Grip of Death: A Study of Modern Money, Debt Slavery and Destructive Economics*, 158–159; see also Chapter 2.

59 Burch and Lawrence, "Towards a Third Food Regime: Behind the Transformation," 275.

60 Kneen, "Restructuring Food for Corporate Profit: The Corporate Genetics of Cargill and Monsanto," 199.

61 Ploeg, *The New Peasantries*.

62 Ibid., 102.

63 Ibid., 257.

64 Brewster Kneen, *Invisible Giant: Cargill and Its Transnational Strategies*, 2nd ed. (London: Pluto Press, 2002), 134 ff.

65 Ploeg, *The New Peasantries*, 95.

66 Rossman, "What Financialization Means for Food Workers," 21.

67 Geoffrey Lawrence and David Burch, "Understanding Supermarkets and Agri-Food Supply Chains," in *Supermarkets and Agri-food Supply Chains*, ed. David Burch and Geoffrey Lawrence (Cheltenham: Edward Elgar, 2007), 8–9.

68 Ibid., 9.

69 David Burch and Geoffrey Lawrence, "Supermarket Own Brands, Supply Chains and the Transformation of the Agri-Food System," *International Journal of Sociology of Agriculture*

and Food 13, no. 1 (2005): 8–9.

70 Ibid.

71 Patel, *Stuffed and Starved*, 220.

72 Ibid., 230.

73 Graeme Willis, *From Field to Fork: The Value of England's Local Food Webs* (London: Campaign to Protect Rural England, June 2012), 33, http://bit.ly/field2fork_cpre (accessed August 4, 2012).

74 Ibid.

75 Patel, *Stuffed and Starved*, 243–244.

76 Ibid., 244.

77 Jane Dixon, "Supermarkets as New Food Authorities," in *Supermarkets and Agri-food Supply Chain*, ed. David Burch and Geoffrey Lawrence (Cheltenham: Edward Elgar, 2007), 31 & 38–39.

78 Lang and Heasman, *Food Wars: the Global Battle for Mouths, Minds and Markets*, 237.

79 Terry K. Marsden and Sarah Whatmore, "Finance Capital and Food System Restructuring: National Incorporation of Global Dynamics," in *The Global Restructuring of Agro-Food Systems*, ed. Philip McMichael (Ithaca: Cornell University Press, 1994), 109.

80 Burch and Lawrence, "Towards a Third Food Regime: Behind the Transformation," 274.

81 Ibid., 276.

82 McMichael, "Global Development and the Corporate Food Regime," 285.

Chapter 6

1 Nina Luttinger and Gregory Dicum, *The Coffee Book: Anatomy of an Industry from Crop to the Last Drop*, 2nd ed. (London: The New Press, 2009), 39–40.

2 Ibid., 25.

3 Atkins and Bowler, *Food in Society*, 23.

4 Luttinger and Dicum, *The Coffee Book: Anatomy of an Industry from Crop to the Last Drop*, 26.

5 John M. Talbot, *Grounds for Agreement: The Political Economy of the Coffee Commodity Chain* (Oxford: Rowman & Littlefield, 2004), 44.

6 With the substitution of market mechanisms for other (colonial) forms of regulation of production and consumption, the possibility for direct involvement of citizens of consumer countries into the "politics" of coffee production (through mediating colonial structures) was severed (Luttinger and Dicum, *The Coffee Book: Anatomy of an Industry from Crop to the Last Drop*, 208). As it will be shown later, this disappearance has left a gap which only recently has started to be filled through the creation of various transnational networks "shortening" the producer-consumer divide, as enacted—for example—by the Fair Trade coffee movement.

7 Friedmann and McMichael, "Agriculture and the State System," 76.

8 Bello, *The Food Wars*, 22; Talbot, *Grounds for Agreement: The Political Economy of the Coffee Commodity Chain*, 43.

9 Robbins, *Stolen Fruit: The Tropical Commodities Disaster*, 62.

10 Benoit Daviron and Stefano Ponte, *The Coffee Paradox: Global Markets, Commodity Trade and the Elusive Promise of Development* (London: Zed Books, 2005), 84.

11 Luttinger and Dicum, *The Coffee Book: Anatomy of an Industry from Crop to the Last Drop*, 75–76.

12 Talbot, *Grounds for Agreement: The Political Economy of the Coffee Commodity Chain*, 63.

13 Daviron and Ponte, *The Coffee Paradox: Global Markets, Commodity Trade and the Elusive Promise of Development*, 85.

14 An early attempt at which was the Inter-American Coffee Agreement between Brasil, Colombia and the United States during the war years (Ibid., 86).

15 David Williams, *International Development and Global Politics* (London: Routledge, 2012).

16 Daviron and Ponte, *The Coffee Paradox: Global Markets, Commodity Trade and the Elusive Promise of Development*, 87.

17 Luttinger and Dicum, *The Coffee Book: Anatomy of an Industry from Crop to the Last Drop*, 53 ff.

18 Ibid., 50.

19 Daviron and Ponte, *The Coffee Paradox: Global Markets, Commodity Trade and the Elusive Promise of Development*, 68.

20 Luttinger and Dicum, *The Coffee Book: Anatomy of an Industry from Crop to the Last Drop*, 92. Roasters, located in consuming countries, buy beans either directly from producers or from a broker and roast them for final consumption (Ibid., 114).

21 Luttinger and Dicum, *The Coffee Book: Anatomy of an Industry from Crop to the Last Drop*, 132.

22 Bill Vorley, *Food, Inc: Corporate Concentration From Farm to Consumer* (London: UK Food Group, 2003), 47–48.

23 International Coffee Organization, "Mission", 2012, http://bit.ly/ICO_mission (accessed July 23, 2012).

24 Llambi, "Opening Economies and Closing Markets: Latin American Agriculture's Difficult Search for a Place in the Emerging Global Order," 189–190.

25 Williams, *International Development and Global Politics*, 115–116; Luttinger and Dicum, *The Coffee Book: Anatomy of an Industry from Crop to the Last Drop*, 94.

26 Vorley, *Food, Inc: Corporate Concentration From Farm to Consumer*, 48.

27 Robbins, *Stolen Fruit: The Tropical Commodities Disaster*, 136.

28 Williams, *International Development and Global Politics*, 111–124.

29 Robbins, *Stolen Fruit: The Tropical Commodities Disaster*, 30.

30 Luttinger and Dicum, *The Coffee Book: Anatomy of an Industry from Crop to the Last Drop*, 97–98.

31 Patel, *Stuffed and Starved*, 9.

32 David Ransom, "The Boat, The Roast and Nutty Mild Colombian," *The New Internationalist*, 1995, http://bit.ly/ransom_coffee (accessed July 23, 2012).

33 Susan A. Newman, "Financialization and Changes in the Social Relations along Commodity Chains: The Case of Coffee," *Review of Radical Political Economics* 41, no. 4 (Fall 2009): 557.

34 Robbins, *Stolen Fruit: The Tropical Commodities Disaster*, 172.

35 Kevin G. Hall, "Got 10 Bucks For a Cup of Joe? Speculators Bid Up Coffee Prices," *McClatchy Washington Bureau* (Washington D.C., August 25, 2011), http://bit.ly/hall_coffee (accessed July 23, 2012).

36 Talbot, "Information, Finance and the New International Inequality: The Case of Coffee," 232.

37 Maarten van der Molen, *Speculators Invading the Commodity Markets: A Case Study of Coffee* (Utrecht: Science Shop of Law, Economics and Governance, Utrecht University, 2009).

38 Newman, "Financialization and Changes in the Social Relations along Commodity Chains: The Case of Coffee," 548; Talbot, "Information, Finance and the New International Inequality: The Case of Coffee," 226.

39 Ghosh, "The Unnatural Coupling: Food and Global Finance," 79; Newman, "Financialization and Changes in the Social Relations along Commodity Chains: The Case of Coffee," 541.

40 Newman, "Financialization and Changes in the Social Relations along Commodity Chains: The Case of Coffee," 550.

41 Llambi, "Opening Economies and Closing Markets: Latin American Agriculture's Difficult Search for a Place in the Emerging Global Order," 190.

42 Ibid.

43 Luttinger and Dicum, *The Coffee Book: Anatomy of an Industry from Crop to the Last Drop*, 139.

44 Daviron and Ponte, *The Coffee Paradox: Global Markets, Commodity Trade and the Elusive Promise of Development*, 57; Luttinger and Dicum, *The Coffee Book: Anatomy of an Industry from Crop to the Last Drop*, 146.

45 Luttinger and Dicum, *The Coffee Book: Anatomy of an Industry from Crop to the Last Drop*, 143.

46 Daviron and Ponte, *The Coffee Paradox: Global Markets, Commodity Trade and the Elusive Promise of Development*, 57.

47 Luttinger and Dicum, *The Coffee Book: Anatomy of an Industry from Crop to the Last Drop*, 156.

48 Ibid., 158.

49 Oliver Strand, "With Coffee, the Price of Individualism Can Be High," *The New York Times*, February 7, 2012, http://bit.ly/strand_NYT (accessed July 23, 2012).

50 Luttinger and Dicum, *The Coffee Book: Anatomy of an Industry from Crop to the Last Drop*, 160.

51 Shade-grown coffee is coffee produced using varieties of coffee that grow in the shade, so that their cultivation does not result in the elimination of an ecosystem that is conducive to the life of several species of migratory birds (Ibid., 141).

52 The "shortening" of the supply chain through direct contact between producers and consumers, regardless of actual distance travelled in space and time, can be one of the features of emerging "short food supply chains" (Henk Renting, Terry K. Marsden, and Jo Banks, "Understanding Alternative Food Networks: Exploring the Role of Short Food Supply Chains in Rural Development," *Environment and Planning A* 35 (2003): 393–411).

53 Sarah Whatmore and Lorraine Thorne, "Nourishing Networks: Alternative Geographies of Food," in *Globalising Food: Agrarian Questions and Global Restructuring*, ed. David Goodman and Michael Watts (London: Routledge, 1997), 295.

54 Luttinger and Dicum, *The Coffee Book: Anatomy of an Industry from Crop to the Last Drop*, 208.

55 Spencer Henson and John Humphrey, "Understanding the Complexities of Private Standards in Global Agri-Food Chains as They Impact Developing Countries," *Journal of Development Studies* 46, no. 9 (2010): 1628–1646.

56 Luttinger and Dicum, *The Coffee Book: Anatomy of an Industry from Crop to the Last Drop*, 206; Talbot, *Grounds for Agreement: The Political Economy of the Coffee Commodity Chain*, 209.

57 Talbot, *Grounds for Agreement: The Political Economy of the Coffee Commodity Chain*, 207.

58 Aimee Shreck, "Resistance, Redistribution and Power in the Fair Trade Banana Initiative," in *The Fight Over Food: Producers, Consumers, and Activists Challenge the Global Food System*, ed. Wynne Wright and Gerard Middendorf (University Park, PA: Pennsylvania State University Press, 2008), 135 & 139.

59 Ibid., 139–140; Daniel Jaffee, *Brewing Justice: Fair Trade Coffee, Sustainability, and Survival* (Berkeley, CA: University of California Press, 2007), 261.

60 Luttinger and Dicum, *The Coffee Book: Anatomy of an Industry from Crop to the Last Drop*, 141.

61 Ibid., 161–162.

62 Jean Baudrillard, *The Consumer Society: Myths and Structures* (London: SAGE, 1998).

63 Luttinger and Dicum, *The Coffee Book: Anatomy of an Industry from Crop to the Last Drop*, 161.

64 Ghosh, "The Unnatural Coupling: Food and Global Finance."

65 Whatmore and Thorne, "Nourishing Networks: Alternative Geographies of Food."

66 Gunther Teubner, "Two Readings of Global Law," in *"Il Diritto del Comune" Seminar* (Turin: International University College & Uninomade, 2011), http://bit.ly/teubner (accessed

July 23, 2012).

67   Bonanno and Constance, *Stories of Globalization: Transnational Corporations, Resistance, and the State*, 9.

Chapter 7

1   Ploeg, *The New Peasantries*, 246.

2   Olivier De Schutter, "How Not to Think of Land-Grabbing: Three Critiques of Large-Scale Investments in Farmland," *Journal of Peasant Studies* 38, no. 2 (2011): 251.

3   S. Haralambous, H. Liversage, and M. Romano, *The Growing Demand for Land Risks and Opportunities for Smallholder Farmers*, Discussion Paper prepared for the Round Table organized during the Thirty-second session of IFAD's Governing Council, 18 February 2009 (Rome: IFAD, 2009), 2.

4   Jennifer Baka, "Biofuels and Wasteland Grabbing: How India's Biofuel Policy is Facilitating Land Grabs in Tamil Nadu, India," in *International Conference on Global Land Grabbing* (Brighton: Land Deal Politics Initiative, 2011), 11, http://bit.ly/baka_grabs (accessed July 23, 2012).

5   Lang, Barling, and Caraher, *Food Policy*, 197.

6   Philip McMichael, "The Land Grab and Corporate Food Regime Restructuring," *Journal of Peasant Studies* 39, no. 3–4 (2012): 683 & 686.

7   Biel, "The Political Economy of Food – Towards an Entropy-Based Systems Analysis of the Current Crisis and Its Solution," 2.

8   Daniel Shepard, "Situating Private Equity Capital in the Land Grab Debate," *Journal of Peasant Studies* 39, no. 3–4 (2012): 714.

9   Lorenzo Cotula et al., *Land Grab or Development Opportunity? Agricultural Investment and International Land Deals in Africa* (London/Rome: IIED/FAO/IFAD, 2009), 17.

10 Prosper B. Matondi and Patience Mutopo, "Attracting Foreign Direct Investment in Africa in the Context of Land

Grabbing for Biofuels and Food Security," in *Biofuels, Land Grabbing and Food Security in Africa*, ed. Prosper B. Matondi, Kjell Havnevik, and Atakilte Beyene (London: Zed Books, 2011), 68–89.

11 McMichael, "The Land Grab and Corporate Food Regime Restructuring," 691–692.

12 Olivier De Schutter and Peter Rosenblum, "Large-Scale Investments in Farmland: The Regulatory Challenge," in *Yearbook on International Investment Law and Policy 2010-11*, ed. Karl P. Sauvant (Oxford: Oxford University Press, 2011), 570.

13 Williams, *International Development and Global Politics*, 37.

14 Bello, *The Food Wars*, 27.

15 McMichael, *Development and Social Change*, 78–79.

16 W. Arthur Lewis, "Economic Development with Unlimited Supplies of Labour," *The Manchester School* 22, no. 2 (May 1, 1954): 139–191.

17 De Schutter and Rosenblum, "Large-Scale Investments in Farmland: The Regulatory Challenge," 570.

18 Robbins, *Stolen Fruit: The Tropical Commodities Disaster*, 29–32.

19 De Schutter and Rosenblum, "Large-Scale Investments in Farmland: The Regulatory Challenge," 570.

20 Klaus Deininger et al., *Rising Global Interest in Farmland: Can It Yield Sustainable and Equitable Benefits?* (Washington D.C.: The World Bank, 2011), xiii, http://bit.ly/deininger (accessed July 23, 2012).

21 Ben White et al., "The New Enclosures: Critical Perspectives on Corporate Land Deals," *Journal of Peasant Studies* 39, no. 3–4 (2012): 626.

22 Williams, *International Development and Global Politics*, 37.

23 Stephanie Black, *Life + Debt*, Documentary (Tuff Gong Pictures, 2001), http://bit.ly/life_debt (accessed July 23, 2012).

24 Prosper B. Matondi, Kjell Havnevik, and Atakilte Beyene, "Conclusion: Land Grabbing, Smallholder Farmers and the Meaning of Agro-Investor-Driven Agrarian Change in Africa," in *Biofuels, Land Grabbing and Food Security in Africa*, ed. Prosper B. Matondi, Kjell Havnevik, and Atakilte Beyene (London: Zed Books, 2011), 180.

25 Tomaso Ferrando, "Land Grabs: How the Law Pushes People Off Their Land," *Pambazuka News*, June 20, 2012, http://bit.ly/ferrando (accessed August 1, 2012).

26 Saturnino M. Borras Jr. and Jennifer Franco, "Regulating Land Grabbing?," *Pambazuka News*, December 16, 2010, http://bit.ly/borras_franco (accessed August 1, 2012).

27 Deininger et al., *Rising Global Interest in Farmland: Can It Yield Sustainable and Equitable Benefits?*, xlii.

28 Ibid.

29 World Bank et al., *Principles for Responsible Agricultural Investment that Respects Rights, Livelihoods and Resources* (FAO/IFAD/UNCTAD/World Bank Group, 2010), http://bit. ly/WB_principles (accessed July 23, 2012).

30 Daniel Ribeiro et al., *The Jatropha Trap? The Realities of Jatropha Farming in Mozambique* (Amsterdam: Friends of the Earth International, May 2010), 5, http://bit.ly/ribeiro_ jatropha (accessed February 26, 2012).

31 Jon R. Luoma, "Hailed as a Miracle Biofuel, Jatropha Falls Short of Hype," *the Guardian*, May 5, 2009, sec. Environment, http://bit.ly/luoma_jatropha (accessed July 23, 2012).

32 McMichael, "The Land Grab and Corporate Food Regime Restructuring," 686.

33 Ribeiro et al., *The Jatropha Trap? The Realities of Jatropha Farming in Mozambique*, 11.

34 Ibid., 13.

35 Ibid., 19.

36 De Schutter and Rosenblum, "Large-Scale Investments in Farmland: The Regulatory Challenge," 604; Klaus Deininger,

"Challenges Posed by the New Wave of Farmland Investment," *Journal of Peasant Studies* 38, no. 2 (2011): 243.

37 De Schutter and Rosenblum, "Large-Scale Investments in Farmland: The Regulatory Challenge," 565.

38 Ribeiro et al., *The Jatropha Trap? The Realities of Jatropha Farming in Mozambique,* 13.

39 Deininger et al., *Rising Global Interest in Farmland: Can It Yield Sustainable and Equitable Benefits?*, xlii.

40 Ribeiro et al., *The Jatropha Trap? The Realities of Jatropha Farming in Mozambique,* 21.

41 Ibid., 16.

42 Soupana Lahiri, "Colonizing the Commons: It Is Jatropha Now!," *Mausam: Taking Climate in Public Space,* September 2008, http://bit.ly/lahiri_jatropha (accessed July 23, 2012).

43 Baka, "Biofuels and Wasteland Grabbing: How India's Biofuel Policy is Facilitating Land Grabs in Tamil Nadu, India," 4.

44 Ibid., 2.

45 Lahiri, "Colonizing the Commons: It Is Jatropha Now!," 15; Prosper B. Matondi, Kjell Havnevik, and Atakilte Beyene, "Introduction: Biofuels, Food Security and Land Grabbing in Africa," in *Biofuels, Land Grabbing and Food Security in Africa,* ed. Prosper B. Matondi, Kjell Havnevik, and Atakilte Beyene (London: Zed Books, 2011), 8.

46 Baka, "Biofuels and Wasteland Grabbing: How India's Biofuel Policy is Facilitating Land Grabs in Tamil Nadu, India," 14.

47 Ibid., 22–23.

48 Michael Levien, "The Land Question: Special Economic Zones and the Political Economy of Dispossession in India," *Journal of Peasant Studies* 39, no. 3–4 (2012): 933–969.

49 De Schutter and Rosenblum, "Large-Scale Investments in Farmland: The Regulatory Challenge," 275.

50 De Schutter, "How not to think of land-grabbing," 256; De

Schutter and Rosenblum, "Large-Scale Investments in Farmland: The Regulatory Challenge," 580.

51 De Schutter, "How not to think of land-grabbing," 267.

52 Ibid., 268; Saturnino M. Borras Jr. and Eric B. Ross, "Land Rights, Conflict, and Violence Amid Neo-Liberal Globalization," *Peace Review* 19, no. 1 (2007): 3.

53 Baka, "Biofuels and Wasteland Grabbing: How India's Biofuel Policy is Facilitating Land Grabs in Tamil Nadu, India," 14.

54 De Schutter, "How not to think of land-grabbing," 271.

55 Jason McLure, "Ethiopian Farms Lure Investor Funds as Workers Live in Poverty," *Bloomberg*, December 30, 2009, http://bit.ly/mclure (accessed July 23, 2012).

56 Matondi, Havnevik, and Beyene, "Conclusion: Land Grabbing, Smallholder Farmers and the Meaning of Agro-Investor-Driven Agrarian Change in Africa," 180.

57 McMichael, "The Land Grab and Corporate Food Regime Restructuring."

58 Ibid., 686 & 697.

59 Biel, "The Political Economy of Food – Towards an Entropy-Based Systems Analysis of the Current Crisis and Its Solution," 4.

60 Holt-Gimenez and Patel, *Food Rebellions*, 96.

61 De Schutter and Rosenblum, "Large-Scale Investments in Farmland: The Regulatory Challenge," 573–574.

Chapter 8

1 Nicholas Georgescu-Roegen, *La décroissance. Entropie – Écologie – Économie*, 2nd ed. (Paris: Éditions Sang de la terre, 1995), 40–41, http://bit.ly/georgescu_roegen (accessed August 23, 2012).

2 Baudrillard, *The Consumer Society*, 175–176.

3 Patel, *The Value of Nothing*, 25 ff.; Charles Taylor, *The Ethics of Authenticity* (Cambridge, MA: Harvard University Press,

1992), 1–12.

4   Don Slater, *Consumer Culture and Modernity* (Cambridge: Polity, 1997), 107.

5   Silvia Federici, *Caliban and the Witch* (Brooklyn, NY: Autonomedia, 2004), 74–75 & 97. Federici also weaves an intriguing explanation of how "witch hunts" actually served the purpose of enforcing these new gender roles, offering spectacular demonizations of those traits (promiscuity and sexual liberation, or avoidance of procreation) that countered the tendency to structure women as a "sink" from which to fuel the new capitalist work relations (Ibid., 184).

6   Goodman and Redclift, *Refashioning Nature: Food, Ecology and Culture*, 75.

7   Federici, *Caliban and the Witch*, 220–229.

8   Ugo Mattei and Laura Nader, *Plunder: When the Rule of Law is Illegal* (Oxford: Wiley-Blackwell, 2008), 31.

9   Meadows, *Thinking in Systems: A Primer*, 145.

10 Norman Long, "Resistance, Agency and Counterwork: A Theoretical Positioning," in *The Fight Over Food: Producers, Consumers, and Activists Challenge the Global Food System*, ed. Wynne Wright and Gerard Middendorf (University Park, PA: Pennsylvania State University Press, 2008), 82–83.

11 Ibid., 76.

12 Gunther Teubner, *Constitutional Fragments: Societal Constitutionalism and Globalization* (Oxford: Oxford University Press, 2012), 83 ff.

13 Ibid., 81.

14 Clapp, *Food*, 177 & 181.

15 De Schutter and Rosenblum, "Large-Scale Investments in Farmland: The Regulatory Challenge," 581.

16 Olivier De Schutter, *Large-Scale Land Acquisitions and Leases: A Set of Minimum Principles and Measures to Address the Human Rights Challenge*, Report of the Special Rapporteur on the right to food (New York: Uited Nations General

Assembly, December 28, 2009), para. 18, http://bit.ly/des chutter (accessed August 4, 2012).

17 Ibid., para. 21.

18 Ibid., para. 26–27.

19 De Schutter, *Food Commodities Speculation and Food Price Crises*, 8.

20 Willis, *From Field to Fork: The Value of England's Local Food Webs*, 60 ff.

21 Teubner, *Constitutional Fragments*, 85.

22 Ibid., 93.

23 Long, "Resistance, Agency and Counterwork: A Theoretical Positioning."

24 Ibid., 84.

25 Ploeg, *The New Peasantries*, 268.

26 Angrisano, *Genuino Clandestino: Movimento di Resistenze Contadine*.

27 Gianluca Brunori, Adanella Rossi, and Vanessa Malandrin, "Co-producing Transition: Innovation Processes in Farms Adhering to Solidarity-Based Purchase Groups (GAS) in Tuscany, Italy," *International Journal of Sociology of Agriculture and Food* 18, no. 1 (2011): 48.

28 Daniel Jaffee and Philip H. Howard, "Corporate Cooptation of Organic and Fair Trade Standards," *Agriculture and Human Values*, no. 27 (2010): 387–399.

29 See Charles Eisenstein, *Sacred Economics: Money, Gift, and Society in the Age of Transition* (Berkeley, CA: Evolver Editions, 2011), 51.

30 Rob Hopkins, *The Transition Handbook: From Oil Dependency to Local Resilience* (Totnes: Green Books, 2008), 134.

31 David Holmgren, *Permaculture: Principles and Pathways Beyond Sustainability* (East Meon: Permanent Publications, 2011); see also Biel, "The Political Economy of Food – Towards an Entropy-Based Systems Analysis of the Current Crisis and Its Solution," 6 ff.

32 Tamzin Pinkerton and Rob Hopkins, *Local Food* (Totnes: Green Books, 2009), 15.

33 Ibid., 47 & 71; see also Biel, "The Political Economy of Food – Towards an Entropy-Based Systems Analysis of the Current Crisis and Its Solution," 10.

34 Pinkerton and Hopkins, *Local Food*, 47; see also E. Piercy, R. Granger, and C. Goodier, "Planning for Peak Oil: Learning From Cuba's 'Special Period'," *Urban Design and Planning* 163, no. DP4 (2010): 172–173.

35 Pinkerton and Hopkins, *Local Food*, 22.

36 Ibid., 103.

37 Willis, *From Field to Fork: The Value of England's Local Food Webs*, 27.

38 The focus on providing local solutions to global problems—which sits at the heart of Transition initiatives—has been criticised both in general (Greg Sharzer, *No Local: Why Small-Scale Alternatives Won't Change the World* (Winchester: Zero Books, 2012)) and with specific reference to the Transition movement (Paul Chatterton and Alice Cutler, *The Rocky Road to a Real Transition: the Transition Towns Movement and What it Means for Social Change* (Leeds: Trapese Collective, 2008), http://bit.ly/trapese2008 (accessed August 2, 2012)). These critiques—coming from authors that are nonetheless sympathetic to local activism—take issue with the lack of willingness to challenge overarching power structures. In response to these, North and Longhurst (Peter North and Noel Longhurst, *Beyond the Rural Idyll: Political Strategies of Urban "Transition" Initiatives*, 3S Working Paper (Norwich: Science, Society and Sustainability Research Group, July 2012), 6, http://bit.ly/north_longhurst (accessed February 8, 2012)) have argued that it is the nature of Transition activism to be "generative" rather than oppositional, stressing "actors' capacities to act, and obstacles as issues to be dealt with, rather than metanarrratives of capitalist

domination." This view stresses the position of Transition initiatives as attempts to shift paradigms, seeking to build new connections that draw resources away from existing power structures so as to eventually make these obsolete (Pinkerton and Hopkins, *Local Food*, 29–30).

39 Ploeg, *The New Peasantries*, 269–270.

40 Ibid., 270.

41 Eisenstein, *Sacred Economics*, 23.

42 Tudge, *Feeding People is Easy*, 95–96.

43 Eisenstein, *Sacred Economics*, 250.

44 Forum for Food Sovereignty, "Declaration of Nyéléni" (Forum for Food Sovereignty, 2007), http://bit.ly/nyeleni (accessed July 23, 2012); La Via Campesina, "Food Sovereignty: A Future Without Hunger" (La Via Campesina, 1996), http://bit.ly/viacampesina_1996 (accessed July 23, 2012).

Bibliography

Altieri, Miguel. *Agroecology: The Science of Sustainable Agriculture.* 2nd ed. London: Intermediate Technology Publications, 1995.

Anderson, Ben, and Paul Harrison. "The Promise of Non-Representational Theories." In *Taking Place: Non-Representational Theories and Geography,* edited by Ben Anderson and Paul Harrison, 1–34. Farnham: Ashgate, 2010.

Anghie, Antony. *Imperialism, Sovereignty and the Making of International Law.* Cambridge: Cambridge University Press, 2004.

Angrisano, Nicola. *Genuino Clandestino: Movimento di Resistenze Contadine.* Documentary. InsuTv, 2011. http://vimeo.com/34322825 (accessed July 23, 2012).

Artisan Forum. *The New Hygiene Regulations and Speciality Food Production.* Dublin: Food Safety Authority of Ireland, August 2005. http://bit.ly/Artisan_Forum (accessed July 26, 2012).

Atkins, Peter, and Ian Bowler. *Food in Society: Economy, Culture, Geography.* London: Arnold, 2001.

Baka, Jennifer. "Biofuels and Wasteland Grabbing: How India's Biofuel Policy is Facilitating Land Grabs in Tamil Nadu, India." In *International Conference on Global Land Grabbing.* Brighton: Land Deal Politics Initiative, 2011. http://bit.ly/baka_grabs (accessed July 23, 2012).

Baudrillard, Jean. *The Consumer Society: Myths and Structures.* London: SAGE, 1998.

Beckert, Jens. *Beyond the Market: The Social Foundations of Economic Efficiency.* Translated by Barbara Harshav. Princeton: Princeton University Press, 2002.

Bello, Walden. *The Food Wars.* London: Verso, 2009.

Bernstein, Henry. " 'The Peasantry' in Global Capitalism: Who, Where and Why?" *Socialist Register* 37 (2001): 25–51.

Biel, Robert. *The Entropy of Capitalism.* Leiden: Brill, 2011.

———. "The Political Economy of Food – Towards an Entropy-Based Systems Analysis of the Current Crisis and Its Solution". Paris: Association Française d'Économie Politique, 2012. http://bit.ly/biel2012 (accessed July 30, 2012).

Bjerga, Alan. "How Goldman Sachs Started the Food Speculation Frenzy." *The Ecologist*, September 13, 2011. http://bit.ly/bjerga _gs (accessed July 23, 2012).

Black, Stephanie. *Life + Debt*. Documentary. Tuff Gong Pictures, 2001. http://bit.ly/life_debt (accessed July 23, 2012).

Blas, Javier. "Commodity Indices: 'Rollover' Practice Hits Investors." *Financial Times*, November 1, 2009. http://bit. ly/blas_roll (accessed July 23, 2012).

Bonanno, Alessandro, and Douglas H. Constance. *Stories of Globalization: Transnational Corporations, Resistance, and the State*. University Park, PA: Pennsylvania State University Press, 2008.

Borgan, Sigmund. "Agricultural Policy in Western Europe and Some of Its Sociological Aspects." *Sociologia Ruralis* 9, no. 3 (1969): 252–260.

Borras, Saturnino M., Jr., and Jennifer Franco. "Regulating Land Grabbing?" *Pambazuka News*, December 16, 2010. http:// bit.ly/borras_franco (accessed August 1, 2012).

Borras, Saturnino M., Jr., and Eric B. Ross. "Land Rights, Conflict, and Violence Amid Neo-Liberal Globalization." *Peace Review* 19, no. 1 (2007): 1–4.

Boyer, Robert. "Capitalism Strikes Back: Why and What Consequences for Social Sciences?" *Revue de la régulation* 1 (2007). http://bit.ly/boyer_2007 (accessed July 25, 2012).

Bradford De Long, J., Andrei Shleifer, Lawrence H. Summers, and Robert J. Waldmann. "Positive Feedback Investment Staregies and Destabilizing Rational Speculation." *The Journal of Finance* 45, no. 2 (June 1990): 379–395.

Brunori, Gianluca, Adanella Rossi, and Vanessa Malandrin. "Co-producing Transition: Innovation Processes in Farms

Adhering to Solidarity-Based Purchase Groups (GAS) in Tuscany, Italy." *International Journal of Sociology of Agriculture and Food* 18, no. 1 (2011): 28–53.

Bryan, Dick, and Michael Rafferty. *Capitalism with Derivatives: A Political Economy of Financial Derivatives, Capital and Class.* Basingstoke: Palgrave Macmillan, 2006.

— — —. "Financial Derivatives and the Theory of Money." *Economy and Society* 36, no. 1 (2007): 134–158.

— — —. "Financial Derivatives: Bubble or Anchor?" In *Global Finance in the New Century*, edited by Libby Assassi, Anastasia Nesvetailova, and Duncan Wigan, 25–37. Basingstoke: Palgrave Macmillan, 2007.

Burch, David, and Geoffrey Lawrence. "Supermarket Own Brands, Supply Chains and the Transformation of the Agri-Food System." *International Journal of Sociology of Agriculture and Food* 13, no. 1 (2005): 1–18.

— — —. "Towards a Third Food Regime: Behind the Transformation." *Agriculture and Human Values* 26 (2009): 267–279.

Carolan, Michael. *The Sociology of Food and Agriculture.* London: Earthscan, 2012.

Chandrasekhar, C.P., and Jayati Ghosh. "Another Looming Food Crisis." *The Hindu Business Line*, July 23, 2012. http://bit.ly/ghosh_chandr (accessed August 3, 2012).

Chatterton, Paul, and Alice Cutler. *The Rocky Road to a Real Transition: the Transition Towns Movement and What it Means for Social Change.* Leeds: Trapese Collective, 2008. http://bit.ly/trapese2008 (accessed August 2, 2012).

Clapp, Jennifer. *Food.* Cambridge: Polity, 2012.

Cotula, Lorenzo, Sonja Vermeulen, Rebeca Leonard, and James Keeley. *Land Grab or Development Opportunity? Agricultural Investment and International Land Deals in Africa.* London/Rome: IIED/FAO/IFAD, 2009.

Daviron, Benoit, and Stefano Ponte. *The Coffee Paradox: Global*

Markets, Commodity Trade and the Elusive Promise of Development. London: Zed Books, 2005.

Deininger, Klaus. "Challenges Posed by the New Wave of Farmland Investment." *Journal of Peasant Studies* 38, no. 2 (2011): 217–247.

Deininger, Klaus, Derek Byerlee, Jonathan Lindsay, Andrew Norton, Harris Selod, and Mercedes Stickler. *Rising Global Interest in Farmland: Can It Yield Sustainable and Equitable Benefits?* Washington D.C.: The World Bank, 2011. http://bit.ly/deininger (accessed July 23, 2012).

Didier, Emmanuel. "Do Statistics 'Perform' the Economy?" In *Do Economists Make Markets? On the Performativity of Economics*, edited by Donald MacKenzie, Fabian Muniesa, and Lucia Siu, 276–310. Princeton: Princeton University Press, 2007.

Dixon, Jane. "Supermarkets as New Food Authorities." In *Supermarkets and Agri-food Supply Chain*, edited by David Burch and Geoffrey Lawrence, 29–50. Cheltenham: Edward Elgar, 2007.

Eisenstein, Charles. *Sacred Economics: Money, Gift, and Society in the Age of Transition.* Berkeley, CA: Evolver Editions, 2011.

Epstein, Gerald A. "Introduction: Financialization and the World Economy." In *Financialization and the World Economy*, edited by Gerald A. Epstein, 3–16. Cheltenham: Edward Elgar, 2006.

Esposito, Elena. *The Future of Futures: The Time of Money in Financing and Society.* Cheltenham: Edward Elgar, 2011.

Fama, Eugene. "Efficient Capital Markets: A Review of Theory and Empirical Work." *Journal of Finance* 25 (1970): 383–417.

Federici, Silvia. *Caliban and the Witch.* Brooklyn, NY: Autonomedia, 2004.

Ferrando, Tomaso. "Land Grabs: How the Law Pushes People Off Their Land." *Pambazuka News*, June 20, 2012. http://bit.ly/ferrando (accessed August 1, 2012).

Fischer-Lescano, Andreas, and Gunther Teubner. "Regime-Collisions: The Vain Search for Legal Unity in the

Fragmentation of Global Law." Translated by Michelle Everson. *Michigan Journal of International Law* 4 (2004): 999–1046.

Forum for Food Sovereignty. "Declaration of Nyéléni". Forum for Food Sovereignty, 2007. http://bit.ly/nyeleni (accessed July 23, 2012).

Foster, John Bellamy. *The Vulnerable Planet: A Short Economic History of the Environment.* New York: Monthly Review Press, 1999.

Frenk, David, and Michael W. Masters. *Anthropic Finance: How Markets Function.* Anthropic Finance and Better Markets: Toward a New Understanding of How Markets Function and the Role They Serve in Society. Washington D.C.: Better Markets, 2010. http://bit.ly/frenk_masters (accessed July 23, 2012).

Frenk, David, and Wallace Turbeville. *Commodity Index Traders and the Boom/Bust Cycle in Commodities Prices.* Anthropic Finance and Better Markets: Toward a New Understanding of How Markets Function and the Role They Serve in Society. Washington D.C.: Better Markets, 2011. http://bit.ly/fr_tur beville (accessed July 23, 2012).

Friedmann, Harriet. "Distance and Durability: Shaky Foundations of the World Food Economy." In *The Global Restructuring of Agro-Food Systems,* edited by Philip McMichael, 258–76. Ithaca: Cornell University Press, 1994.

Friedmann, Harriet, and Philip McMichael. "Agriculture and the State System." *Sociologia Ruralis* 29, no. 2 (1989): 73–117.

Gallino, Luciano. *Finanzcapitalismo: La Civiltà del Denaro in Crisi.* Turin: Einaudi, 2011.

Ganesh, Aravind. "The Right to Food and Buyer Power." *German Law Journal* 11, no. 11 (2010): 1190–1244.

Garner, Carley. *A Trader's First Book on Commodities.* Upper Saddle River, NJ: FT Press, 2010.

Georgescu-Roegen, Nicholas. *La décroissance. Entropie – Écologie –*

Économie. 2nd ed. Paris: Éditions Sang de la terre, 1995. http://bit.ly/georgescu_roegen (accessed August 23, 2012).

Ghosh, Jayati. *Commodity Speculation and the Food Crisis*. Briefing. World Development Movement, October 2010. http://bit.ly/ghosh_wdm (accessed July 23, 2012).

— — —. "The Unnatural Coupling: Food and Global Finance." *Journal of Agrarian Change* 10, no. 1 (2010): 72–86.

Girelli, Giuliano. *The Last Farmer*. Documentary. M.A.I.S. ong, 2012. http://vimeo.com/38351098 (accessed July 23, 2012).

Goodman, David, and Michael Redclift. *Refashioning Nature: Food, Ecology and Culture*. London: Routledge, 1991.

Goodman, David, Bernardo Sorj, and John Wilkinson. *From Farming to Biotechnology: A Theory of Agro-Industrial Development*. Oxford: Blackwell, 1987.

Greer, Robert J. "The Nature of Commodity Index Returns." *The Journal of Alternative Investments* 3, no. 1 (2000): 45–53.

Hall, Kevin G. "Got 10 Bucks For a Cup of Joe? Speculators Bid Up Coffee Prices." *McClatchy Washington Bureau*. Washington D.C., August 25, 2011. http://bit.ly/hall_coffee (accessed July 23, 2012).

Haralambous, S., H. Liversage, and M. Romano. *The Growing Demand for Land Risks and Opportunities for Smallholder Farmers*. Discussion Paper prepared for the Round Table organized during the Thirty-second session of IFAD's Governing Council, 18 February 2009. Rome: IFAD, 2009.

Hardt, Michael, and Antonio Negri. *Empire*. Cambridge, MA: Harvard University Press, 2001.

Harriss, John. *Rural Development: Theories of Peasant Economy and Agrarian Change*. London: Hutchinson, 1982.

Henson, Spencer, and John Humphrey. "Understanding the Complexities of Private Standards in Global Agri-Food Chains as They Impact Developing Countries." *Journal of Development Studies* 46, no. 9 (2010): 1628–1646.

Hessling, Alexandra, and Hanno Pahl. "The Global System of

Finance: Scanning Talcott Parsons and Niklas Luhmann for Theoretical Keystones." *American Journal of Economics and Sociology* 65, no. 1 (2006): 189–218.

Ho, Karen. "Disciplining Investment Bankers, Disciplining the Economy: Wall Street's Institutional Culture of Crisis and the Downsizing of American Corporations." *American Anthropologist* 111, no. 2 (2009): 177–189.

Hobbes, Thomas. *Leviathan or the Matter, Forme & Power of a Commonwealth Ecclesiasticall and Civil*. London: Andrew Cooke, 1651. http://bit.ly/hobbes_leviath (accessed July 23, 2012).

Holmgren, David. *Permaculture: Principles and Pathways Beyond Sustainability*. East Meon: Permanent Publications, 2011.

Holt-Gimenez, Eric, and Raj Patel. *Food Rebellions: Crisis and the Hunger for Justice*. Oxford: Pambazuka Press, 2009.

Hopkins, Rob. *The Transition Handbook: From Oil Dependency to Local Resilience*. Totnes: Green Books, 2008.

Ingham, Geoffrey. *Capitalism*. Cambridge: Polity, 2008.

International Coffee Organization. "Mission", 2012. http://bit.ly/ICO_mission (accessed July 23, 2012).

Irwin, Scott H., Dwight R. Sanders, and Robert P. Merrin. "Devil or Angel? The Role of Speculation in the Recent Commodity Price Boom (and Bust)." *Journal of Agricultural and Applied Economics* 41, no. 2 (August 2009): 377–391.

IUF. *Feeding Financial Markets: Financialization and Restructuring in Nestlé, Kraft and Unilever*. International Union of Food, Agricultural, Hotel, Restaurant, Catering, Tobacco and Allied Workers' Associations, October 2006. http://bit.ly/IUF_finance (accessed July 23, 2012).

Jaffee, Daniel. *Brewing Justice: Fair Trade Coffee, Sustainability, and Survival*. Berkeley, CA: University of California Press, 2007.

Jaffee, Daniel, and Philip H. Howard. "Corporate Cooptation of Organic and Fair Trade Standards." *Agriculture and Human Values*, no. 27 (2010): 387–399.

Kaufman, Frederick. "The Food Bubble: How Wall Street Starved Millions and Got Away With It." *Harper's Magazine*, July 2010.

Kerckhoffs, Thijs, Roos van Os, and Myriam Vander Stichele. *Financing Food: Financialisation and Financial Actors in Agriculture Commodity Markets*. SOMO Paper. Amsterdam: Centre for Research on Multinational Corporations, April 2010. http://bit.ly/kerckhoffs (accessed July 23, 1923).

Kneen, Brewster. *Invisible Giant: Cargill and Its Transnational Strategies*. 2nd ed. London: Pluto Press, 2002.

— — —. "Restructuring Food for Corporate Profit: The Corporate Genetics of Cargill and Monsanto." *Agriculture and Human Values* 16, no. 2 (1999): 161–167.

Knorr Cetina, Karin, and Urs Bruegger. "Global Microstructures: The Virtual Societies of Financial Markets." *American Journal of Sociology* 107, no. 4 (2002): 905–950.

Krippner, Greta R. "The Financialization of the American Economy." *Socio-Economic Review* 3 (2005): 173–208.

Kurtzman, Joel. *The Death of Money*. New York: Simon & Schuster, 1993.

Lahiri, Soupana. "Colonizing the Commons: It Is Jatropha Now!" *Mausam: Taking Climate in Public Space*, September 2008. http://bit.ly/lahiri_jatropha (accessed July 23, 2012).

Lang, Tim, David Barling, and Martin Caraher. *Food Policy: Integrating Health, Environment and Society*. Oxford: Oxford University Press, 2009.

Lang, Tim, and Michael Heasman. *Food Wars: the Global Battle for Mouths, Minds and Markets*. London: Earthscan, 2004.

Latour, Bruno. *Reassembling the Social: An Introduction to Actor-Network Theory*. Oxford: Oxford University Press, 2005.

Laughton, Rebecca. *Surviving and Thriving on the Land*. Totnes: Green Books, 2008.

Lawrence, Geoffrey, and David Burch. "Understanding Supermarkets and Agri-Food Supply Chains." In *Supermarkets and Agri-food Supply Chains*, edited by David Burch and

Geoffrey Lawrence, 1–26. Cheltenham: Edward Elgar, 2007.

Levien, Michael. "The Land Question: Special Economic Zones and the Political Economy of Dispossession in India." *Journal of Peasant Studies* 39, no. 3-4 (2012): 933–969.

Lewis, W. Arthur. "Economic Development with Unlimited Supplies of Labour." *The Manchester School* 22, no. 2 (May 1, 1954): 139–191.

Leyshon, Andrew, and Nigel Thrift. *Money/Space: Geographies of Monetary Transformation*. London: Routledge, 1997.

Lines, Thomas. *Making Poverty: A History*. London: Zed Books, 2008.

— — —. *Speculation in Food Commodity Markets*. World Development Movement, April 2010. http://bit.ly/lines_commodity (accessed July 23, 2012).

LiPuma, Edward, and Benjamin Lee. *Financial Derivatives and the Globalization of Risk*. Durham & London: Duke University Press, 2004.

— — —. "Financial Derivatives and the Rise of Circulation." *Economy and Society* 34, no. 3 (2005): 404–427.

Llambi, Luis. "Opening Economies and Closing Markets: Latin American Agriculture's Difficult Search for a Place in the Emerging Global Order." In *From Columbus to ConAgra: The Globalization of Agriculture and Food*, edited by Alessandro Bonanno, Lawrence Busch, William Friedland, Lourdes Gouveia, and Enzo Mingione, 184–209. Lawrence: University Press of Kansas, 1994.

Long, Norman. "Resistance, Agency and Counterwork: A Theoretical Positioning." In *The Fight Over Food: Producers, Consumers, and Activists Challenge the Global Food System*, edited by Wynne Wright and Gerard Middendorf, 69–89. University Park, PA: Pennsylvania State University Press, 2008.

Luhmann, Niklas. *Ecological Communication*. Translated by John Jr. Bednarz. Chicago: University of Chicago Press, 1989.

———. "Operational Closure and Structural Coupling: the Differentiation of the Legal System." *Cardozo Law Review* 13 (1991-92): 1419–1442.

Luoma, Jon R. "Hailed as a Miracle Biofuel, Jatropha Falls Short of Hype." *the Guardian*, May 5, 2009, sec. Environment. http://bit.ly/luoma_jatropha (accessed July 23, 2012).

Luttinger, Nina, and Gregory Dicum. *The Coffee Book: Anatomy of an Industry from Crop to the Last Drop*. 2nd ed. London: The New Press, 2009.

MacKenzie, Donald. "Is Economics Performative? Option Theory and the Construction of Derivatives Markets." In *Do Economists Make Markets? On the Performativity of Economics*, edited by Donald MacKenzie, Fabian Muniesa, and Lucia Siu, 54–86. Princeton: Princeton University Press, 2007.

———. *Material Markets: How Economic Agents are Constructed*. Oxford: Oxford University Press, 2008.

Macy, Joanna. *Mutual Causality in Buddhism and General Systems Theory*. Albany: State University of New York Press, 1991.

Marazzi, Christian. *The Violence of Financial Capitalism*. Translated by Kristina Lebedeva and Jason Francis McGimsey. Boston: Semiotext(e), 2011.

Marsden, Terry K., and Sarah Whatmore. "Finance Capital and Food System Restructuring: National Incorporation of Global Dynamics." In *The Global Restructuring of Agro-Food Systems*, edited by Philip McMichael. Ithaca: Cornell University Press, 1994.

Masters, Michael W., and Adam K. White. *How Institutional Investors Are Driving Up Food And Energy Prices*. Special Report. The Accidental Hunt Brothers, July 31, 2008. http://bit.ly/masters_white (accessed July 23, 2012).

Matondi, Prosper B., Kjell Havnevik, and Atakilte Beyene. "Conclusion: Land Grabbing, Smallholder Farmers and the Meaning of Agro-Investor-Driven Agrarian Change in Africa." In *Biofuels, Land Grabbing and Food Security in Africa*, edited by

Prosper B. Matondi, Kjell Havnevik, and Atakilte Beyene, 176–195. London: Zed Books, 2011.

― ― ―. "Introduction: Biofuels, Food Security and Land Grabbing in Africa." In *Biofuels, Land Grabbing and Food Security in Africa*, edited by Prosper B. Matondi, Kjell Havnevik, and Atakilte Beyene, 1–19. London: Zed Books, 2011.

Matondi, Prosper B., and Patience Mutopo. "Attracting Foreign Direct Investment in Africa in the Context of Land Grabbing for Biofuels and Food Security." In *Biofuels, Land Grabbing and Food Security in Africa*, edited by Prosper B. Matondi, Kjell Havnevik, and Atakilte Beyene, 68–89. London: Zed Books, 2011.

Mattei, Ugo, and Laura Nader. *Plunder: When the Rule of Law is Illegal*. Oxford: Wiley-Blackwell, 2008.

McLure, Jason. "Ethiopian Farms Lure Investor Funds as Workers Live in Poverty." *Bloomberg*, December 30, 2009. http://bit.ly/mclure (accessed July 23, 2012).

McMichael, Philip. *Development and Social Change*. 4th ed. Los Angeles: Pine Forge Press, 2008.

― ― ―. "Global Development and the Corporate Food Regime." In *New Directions in the Sociology of Global Development*, edited by Frederick H. Buttel and Philip McMichael, 11:269–303. Research in Rural Sociology and Development. Amsterdam: Elsevier, 2005. http://bit.ly/mcmichael_2005 (accessed July 23, 2012).

― ― ―. "The Land Grab and Corporate Food Regime Restructuring." *Journal of Peasant Studies* 39, no. 3-4 (2012): 681–701.

McMichael, Philip, and Harriet Friedmann. "Situating the 'Retailing Revolution'." In *Supermarkets and Agri-Food Supply Chains*, edited by David Burch and Geoffrey Lawrence, 291–319. Cheltenham: Edward Elgar, 2007.

Meadows, Donella H. *Thinking in Systems: A Primer*. Edited by

Diana Wright. London: Earthscan, 2009.

de Medeiros Carneiro, Ricardo, Marcos Vinicius Chiliatto-Leite, Guilherme Santos Mello, and Pedro Rossi. "The Fourth Dimension: Derivatives in a Capitalism With Financial Dominance". Paris: Association Française d'Économie Politique, 2012. http://bit.ly/fourth_dimension (accessed August 13, 2012).

Meulen, Bernd van der. *Reconciling Food Law to Competitiveness: Report of the Regulatory Environment of the European Food and Dairy Sector.* Wageningen: Wageningen Academic Publishers, 2009.

Miéville, China. "The Commodity-Form Theory of International Law." In *International Law on the Left: Re-Examining Marxist Legacies*, edited by Susan Marks, 92–132. Cambridge: Cambridge University Press, 2008.

Moeller, Hans-Georg. *Luhmann Explained: From Souls to Systems.* Peru, IL: Open Court, 2006.

Molen, Maarten van der. *Speculators Invading the Commodity Markets: A Case Study of Coffee.* Utrecht: Science Shop of Law, Economics and Governance, Utrecht University, 2009.

Mou, Yiqun. "Limits to Arbitrage and Commodity Index Investment". PhD Dissertation, New York: Columbia University, 2011. http://bit.ly/mou_2011 (accessed July 23, 2012).

Nesvetailova, Anastasia. *Financial Alchemy in Crisis: The Great Liquidity Illusion.* London: Pluto Press, 2010.

— — —. *Fragile Finance: Debt, Speculation and Crisis in the Age of Global Credit.* Basingstoke: Palgrave Macmillan, 2007.

Newman, Susan A. "Financialization and Changes in the Social Relations along Commodity Chains: The Case of Coffee." *Review of Radical Political Economics* 41, no. 4 (Fall 2009): 539–559.

North, Peter, and Noel Longhurst. *Beyond the Rural Idyll: Political Strategies of Urban "Transition" Initiatives.* 3S Working Paper.

Norwich: Science, Society and Sustainability Research Group, July 2012. http://bit.ly/north_longhurst (accessed February 8, 2012).

Pahl, Hanno. "On the Unity and Difference of Finance and the Economy: Investigations for a New Sociology of Money." In *Towards a Cognitive Mode in Global Finance: The Governance of a Knowledge-based Financial System*, edited by Torsten Strulik and Helmut Willke, 71–104. Frankfurt/New York: Campus, 2006.

Patel, Raj. *Stuffed and Starved*. London: Portobello Books, 2007.

— — —. *The Value of Nothing: How to Reshape Market Society and Redefine Democracy*. London: Portobello Books, 2010.

Peck, Anne E. "The Economic Role of Traditional Commodity Futures Markets." In *Futures Markets: Their Economic Role*, edited by Anne E. Peck, 1–81. Washington D.C.: American Enterprise Institute for Public Policy Research, 1985.

Piercy, E., R. Granger, and C. Goodier. "Planning for Peak Oil: Learning From Cuba's 'Special Period'." *Urban Design and Planning* 163, no. DP4 (2010): 169–176.

Pinkerton, Tamzin, and Rob Hopkins. *Local Food*. Totnes: Green Books, 2009.

Ploeg, Jan Douwe van der. *The New Peasantries: Struggles for Autonomy and Sustainability in an Era of Empire and Globalization*. London: Earthscan, 2009.

Ransom, David. "The Boat, The Roast and Nutty Mild Colombian." *The New Internationalist*, 1995. http://bit.ly/ransom_coffee (accessed July 23, 2012).

Renting, Henk, Terry K. Marsden, and Jo Banks. "Understanding Alternative Food Networks: Exploring the Role of Short Food Supply Chains in Rural Development." *Environment and Planning A* 35 (2003): 393–411.

Ribeiro, Daniel, Nilza Matavel, União Nacional de Camponeses, and Friends of the Earth Mozambique/Justiça Ambiental. *The Jatropha Trap? The Realities of Jatropha Farming in Mozambique*.

Amsterdam: Friends of the Earth International, May 2010. http://bit.ly/ribeiro_jatropha (accessed February 26, 2012).

Robbins, Peter. *Stolen Fruit: The Tropical Commodities Disaster.* London: Zed Books, 2003.

— — —. "Tropical Commodities as Tradeable Assets: An Interview with Peter Robbins." Interview by Luigi Russi, March 26, 2012. http://bit.ly/robbins_interv (accessed July 23, 2012).

Rossman, Peter. "What Financialization Means for Food Workers." *Seedling,* 2010.

Rossman, Peter, and Gerard Greenfield. "Financialization: New Routes to Profit, New Challenges for Trade Unions." *Labour Education* 142, no. 1 (2006). http://bit.ly/rossman_greenfield (accessed July 23, 2012).

Rotman, Brian. *Signifying Nothing: The Semiotics of Zero.* Stanford: Stanford University Press, 1993.

Rowbotham, Michael. *The Grip of Death: A Study of Modern Money, Debt Slavery and Destructive Economics.* Charlbury: Jon Carpenter, 1998.

Salento, Angelo, and Giovanni Masino. "Financialization and Organizational Change: A Comparative Study on Multinational Enterprises." In *CMS7 2011 7th International Critical Management Studies Conference Proceedings.* Naples: Faculty of Economics, University of Naples Federico II, 2011. http://bit.ly/salento_masino (accessed July 23, 2012).

Schrage, Michael D. *Serious Play: How the World's Best Companies Simulate to Innovate.* Cambridge, MA: Harvard Business School Press, 2000.

De Schutter, Olivier. *Food Commodities Speculation and Food Price Crises.* Briefing Note. UN Special Rapporteur on the Right to Food, September 2010.

— — —. "How Not to Think of Land-Grabbing: Three Critiques of Large-Scale Investments in Farmland." *Journal of Peasant Studies* 38, no. 2 (2011): 249–279.

— — —. *Large-Scale Land Acquisitions and Leases: A Set of Minimum Principles and Measures to Address the Human Rights Challenge*. Report of the Special Rapporteur on the right to food. New York: Uited Nations General Assembly, December 28, 2009. http://bit.ly/deschutter (accessed August 4, 2012).

De Schutter, Olivier, and Peter Rosenblum. "Large-Scale Investments in Farmland: The Regulatory Challenge." In *Yearbook on International Investment Law and Policy 2010-11*, edited by Karl P. Sauvant, 563–610. Oxford: Oxford University Press, 2011.

Seidl, David. *Luhmann's Theory of Autopoietic Social Systems*. Working Paper. Munich: Munich School of Management, 2004. http://bit.ly/seidl2004 (accessed January 8, 2012).

Sharzer, Greg. *No Local: Why Small-Scale Alternatives Won't Change the World*. Winchester: Zero Books, 2012.

Shepard, Daniel. "Situating Private Equity Capital in the Land Grab Debate." *Journal of Peasant Studies* 39, no. 3-4 (2012): 703–29.

Shiva, Vandana. *Stolen Harvest: The Hijacking of the Global Food Supply*. Cambridge, MA: South End Press, 1999.

Shreck, Aimee. "Resistance, Redistribution and Power in the Fair Trade Banana Initiative." In *The Fight Over Food: Producers, Consumers, and Activists Challenge the Global Food System*, edited by Wynne Wright and Gerard Middendorf, 121–144. University Park, PA: Pennsylvania State University Press, 2008.

Slater, Don. *Consumer Culture and Modernity*. Cambridge: Polity, 1997.

Sollis, Robert. *Empirical Finance for Finance and Banking*. Chichester: Wiley, 2012.

Soros, George. *The Alchemy of Finance: Reading the Mind of the Market*. New York: John Wiley & Sons, 1994.

— — —. *The New Paradigm for Financial Markets: The Credit Crisis of 2008 and What It Means*. New York: PublicAffairs, 2008.

Staritz, Cornelia. *Financial Markets and the Commodity Price Boom: Causes and Implications for Developing Countries*. Vienna: Oesterreichische Forschungsstiftung fuer Internationale Entwicklung, April 2012. http://bit.ly/staritz (accessed July 23, 2012).

Strand, Oliver. "With Coffee, the Price of Individualism Can Be High." *The New York Times*, February 7, 2012. http://bit.ly/strand_NYT (accessed July 23, 2012).

Talbot, John M. *Grounds for Agreement: The Political Economy of the Coffee Commodity Chain*. Oxford: Rowman & Littlefield, 2004.

— — —. "Information, Finance and the New International Inequality: The Case of Coffee." *Journal of World-Systems Research* 8, no. 2 (2002): 214–250.

Taylor, Charles. *The Ethics of Authenticity*. Cambridge, MA: Harvard University Press, 1992.

Terranova, Tiziana. "New Economy, Financialization and Social Production in the Web 2.0." In *Crisis in the Global Economy: Financial Markets, Social Struggles and New Political Scenarios*, edited by Andrea Fumagalli and Sandro Mezzadra, translated by Jason Francis McGimsey, 153–170. Los Angeles: Semiotext(e), 2010.

Teubner, Gunther. "A Constitutional Moment? The Logics of 'Hitting the Bottom'." In *The Financial Crisis in Constitutional Perspective*, edited by Poul Kjaer, Gunther Teubner, and Alberto Febbrajo. Oxford: Hart Publishing, 2011.

— — —. *Constitutional Fragments: Societal Constitutionalism and Globalization*. Oxford: Oxford University Press, 2012.

— — —. "The Anonymous Matrix: Human Rights Violations by 'Private' Transnational Actors." *Modern Law Review* 69, no. 3 (2006): 327–346.

— — —. "Two Readings of Global Law." In *"Il Diritto del Comune" Seminar*. Turin: International University College & Uninomade, 2011. http://bit.ly/teubner (accessed July 23, 2012).

Thorat, Amit. *Rising Market Control of Transnational Agribusiness*. Focus. New Delhi: International Development Economics Associates, 2003. http://bit.ly/thorat_TNCs (accessed July 23, 2012).

Thrift, Nigel. *Knowing Capitalism*. London: SAGE, 2005.

Trebilcock, Michael J., and Robert Howse. *The Regulation of International Trade*. 2nd ed. London: Routledge, 1999.

Tudge, Colin. *Feeding People is Easy*. Pari: Pari Publishing, 2007.

United Nations Commission on Trade and Development Secretariat. *Price Formation in Financialized Commodity Markets: The Role of Information*. New York-Geneva: United Nations, June 2011.

Varoufakis, Yanis, Joseph Halevi, and Nicholas Theocarakis. *Modern Political Economics: Making Sense of the Post-2008 World*. London: Routledge, 2011.

La Via Campesina. "Food Sovereignty: A Future Without Hunger". La Via Campesina, 1996. http://bit.ly/viacampesina_1996 (accessed July 23, 2012).

———. *Sustainable Peasant and Family Farm Agriculture Can Feed the World*. Jakarta: La Via Campesina, September 2010. http://bit.ly/viacampesina_2010 (accessed July 23, 2012).

Viskovatoff, Alex. "Foundations of Niklas Luhmann's Theory of Social Systems." *Philosophy of the Social Sciences* 29, no. 4 (1999): 481–516.

Vorley, Bill. *Food, Inc: Corporate Concentration From Farm to Consumer*. London: UK Food Group, 2003.

Ward, Neil. "The Agricultural Treadmill and the Rural Environment in the Post-Productivist Era." *Sociologia Ruralis* 33, no. 3-4 (1993): 348–364.

Weis, Anthony. "The Accelerating Biophysical Contradictions of Industrial Capitalist Agriculture." *Journal of Agrarian Change* 10, no. 3 (July 2010): 315–341.

———. *The Global Food Economy: The Battle for the Future of Farming*. London: Zed Books, 2007.

Whatmore, Sarah, and Lorraine Thorne. "Nourishing Networks: Alternative Geographies of Food." In *Globalising Food: Agrarian Questions and Global Restructuring*, edited by David Goodman and Michael Watts, 287–304. London: Routledge, 1997.

White, Ben, Saturnino M. Borras, Ruth Hall, Ian Scoones, and Wendy Wolford. "The New Enclosures: Critical Perspectives on Corporate Land Deals." *Journal of Peasant Studies* 39, no. 3-4 (2012): 619–647.

Wigan, Duncan. "Financialisation and Derivatives: The Political Construction of an Artifice of Indifference." *Competition and Change* 13, no. 2 (2009): 159–174.

Williams, David. *International Development and Global Politics.* London: Routledge, 2012.

Willis, Graeme. *From Field to Fork: The Value of England's Local Food Webs.* London: Campaign to Protect Rural England, June 2012. http://bit.ly/field2fork_cpre (accessed August 4, 2012).

Willke, Helmut. "The Autonomy of the Financial System: Symbolic Coupling and the Language of Capital." In *Towards a Cognitive Mode in Global Finance: The Governance of a Knowledge-based Financial System*, edited by Torsten Strulik and Helmut Willke, 37–70. Frankfurt/New York: Campus Verlag, 2006.

Windawi, A. Jason. *Speculation, Embedding and Food Prices: A Cointegration Analysis.* Working Paper. Institute for Social and Economic Research and Policy. New York: Columbia University, February 2012. http://bit.ly/windawi (accessed July 23, 2012).

World Bank, FAO, IFAD, and UNCTAD. *Principles for Responsible Agricultural Investment that Respects Rights, Livelihoods and Resources.* FAO/IFAD/UNCTAD/World Bank Group, 2010. http://bit.ly/WB_principles (accessed July 23, 2012).

Ziegler, Jean. *Destruction Massive: Géopolitique de la Faim.* Paris: Seuil, 2011.

Select Index

Contemporary culture has eliminated both the concept of the public and the figure of the intellectual. Former public spaces – both physical and cultural – are now either derelict or colonized by advertising. A cretinous anti-intellectualism presides, cheerled by expensively educated hacks in the pay of multinational corporations who reassure their bored readers that there is no need to rouse themselves from their interpassive stupor. The informal censorship internalized and propagated by the cultural workers of late capitalism generates a banal conformity that the propaganda chiefs of Stalinism could only ever have dreamt of imposing. Zer0 Books knows that another kind of discourse – intellectual without being academic, popular without being populist – is not only possible: it is already flourishing, in the regions beyond the striplit malls of so-called mass media and the neurotically bureaucratic halls of the academy. Zer0 is committed to the idea of publishing as a making public of the intellectual. It is convinced that in the unthinking, blandly consensual culture in which we live, critical and engaged theoretical reflection is more important than ever before.